Mazzy Star's So Tonight That I Might See

Anthony Gomez III

BLOOMSBURY ACADEMIC
LONDON • NEW YORK • OXFORD • NEW DELHI • SYDNEY

BLOOMSBURY ACADEMIC
Bloomsbury Publishing Inc, 1359 Broadway, New York, NY 10018, USA
Bloomsbury Publishing Plc, 50 Bedford Square, London, WC1B 3DP, UK
Bloomsbury Publishing Ireland, 29 Earlsfort Terrace, Dublin 2, D02 AY28, Ireland

BLOOMSBURY, BLOOMSBURY ACADEMIC and the Diana logo are
trademarks of Bloomsbury Publishing Plc

First published in the United States of America 2026

Copyright © Anthony Gomez III, 2026

For legal purposes the Acknowledgments on p.viii constitute
an extension of this copyright page.

All rights reserved. No part of this publication may be: i) reproduced or transmitted in any form, electronic or mechanical, including photocopying, recording or by means of any information storage or retrieval system without prior permission in writing from the publishers; or ii) used or reproduced in any way for the training, development or operation of artificial intelligence (AI) technologies, including generative AI technologies. The rights holders expressly reserve this publication from the text and data mining exception as per Article 4(3) of the Digital Single Market Directive (EU) 2019/790.

Bloomsbury Publishing Inc does not have any control over, or responsibility for, any third-party websites referred to or in this book. All internet addresses given in this book were correct at the time of going to press. The author and publisher regret any inconvenience caused if addresses have changed or sites have ceased to exist, but can accept no responsibility for any such changes.

A catalog record for this book is available from the Library of Congress

ISBN: PB: 979-8-7651-3355-2
ePDF: 979-8-7651-3357-6
eBook: 979-8-7651-3358-3

Series: 33 1/3

Typeset by Deanta Global Publishing Services, Chennai, India
Printed and bound in the United States of America

For product safety related questions contact productsafety@bloomsbury.com.

To find out more about our authors and books visit www.bloomsbury.com
and sign up for our newsletters.

For the quiet ones

"All profound things and emotions of things are preceded and amended by Silence, and Silence is the consecration of the universe"—*Herman Melville, from* Pierre, or, The Ambiguities

Contents

Acknowledgments viii

Introduction 1
Fade into You 9
Bells Ring 31
Wasted 53
So Tonight That I Might See 79
Conclusion 99

References 107
Notes 117

Acknowledgments

This book was conceived years ago, but I was too timid to take the plunge and submit a proposal during 33 1/3's annual open call. For pushing me out of the comfort of that simple dream of wanting to discuss and write about the importance of this band to me, I thank my wife Shea, who also endured countless repetitive hours of my working through thoughts and feelings about what belonged and did not belong on the page.

There are many others who helped this project reach its end. While there are far too many friends, colleagues, and students to name, I would like to thank Connor Sedlacek, Kirk Cooper-Johnson, and Anthony Calamunci for asking questions and anticipating polished versions of the manuscript. Michael Tondre at Stony Brook University offered positive assurance about the writing process. I am also grateful that I belong to a community of helpful critics and professors in the English department at the University of Oklahoma.

I feel one should always think about the various communities that have made one's life possible. For that reason, I dedicate this book to my mother, whose stories about growing up in Los Angeles, attending concerts, and discovering new and interesting bands in the city still fascinate me.

Finally, as I mentioned in Chapter 2, stories circulate about Hope Sandoval's frustration with school administrators and teachers who failed to understand her intense shyness. Sometimes, us introverted kids just need a bit of patience. Sometimes, us introverted kids need calm. And so, I also would like to thank the many individuals, forgotten and not forgotten, who offered me patience and calm when I most needed it.

Introduction

Shyness can grate on people the wrong way. It is always a single beat, a second, or a moment away from being received as rude. Today's social media-saturated era has only worsened this tendency. Too many expect artists to offer proximity in return for fandom—however false this proximity may appear. We forget about the power in artists who are simply quiet. Of those who possess restraint. Of those who let their art speak for them and wield introversion like a weapon, sharpening their production with an unparalleled weight. Few artists achieve this power. Fewer artists possess the poise required to sustain it. Creatives who willingly, or unwillingly, choose reclusion imbue their art with intrigue—a too-rare trait. Such is the reason a new publication from Elena Ferrante or Donna Tartt is cause for unfathomable excitement. Or that D'Angelo's return to music with *Black Messiah*, fourteen years since his prior album release, became a noteworthy event. How many pore over the lyrics of *In the Aeroplane over the Sea* to unearth explanations as to why Neutral Milk Hotel's Jeff Mangum vanished from the limelight? Quietness, of course, is not always tied to mental struggle. Private artists, simply put, seem cool. Unburdened by the social pressures of stardom, they go on with their lives. In the process, they hypnotize and tease us with all that we do not know and never will. Don't we still wonder why Greta Garbo retired from acting? Don't we question what J. D. Salinger worked on when he stopped publishing? Don't we also ask if Frank Ocean is producing any new material?

Shyness and silence are the key elements of Mazzy Star's mythology. Silence punctuates the turns in the narrative and their traceable resonances in contemporary music. That a band would sacrifice fame and mainstream success to release the music they wanted when they wanted; that two members from opposite sides of Los Angeles would reject exposure and fame; and that an alternative band at the height of nineties aggression and angst made music for the twilight hours, for the introverts and dreamers are all the ingredients that gave Mazzy Star the intangible excellence so many artists aspire to. Dare I say that dreaded word? It gave them authenticity. Like The Smiths, The Replacements, Nick Drake, or Lauryn Hill, few would accuse Mazzy Star of having "sold out." They seemingly escaped capitalism's pressures by wielding their quiet natures as a force for power and charm.

Shyness and silence were on display when Mazzy Star previewed their sophomore album *So Tonight That I Might See* just over a month before its official release on October 5, 1993. In the confines of the intimate Los Angeles blues venue The Mint, the band finished their set, and the audience's immediate reaction disappointed Hope Sandoval. Not *because* they booed. *Because* they cheered. "Why are you clapping?" the singer snapped over the booming applause. "You weren't even listening."[1]

INTRODUCTION

In his column for *Rolling Stone*, David Wild reacts with curiosity, as if unable to decide whether he admires or disapproves of the exchange. But to Mazzy Star's faithful listeners, this infamous question and declaration from the band's lead singer explain a philosophy behind the album and the band. David Roback and Hope Sandoval spurned the spotlight. Shadows covered them onstage. They ignored the fact people paid to see them and withdrew into their private worlds. They encouraged stillness from crowds to maintain this fragile state. Do not watch. Open your ears. Because to focus on the music—to truly listen—is to find a refuge from humanity's habit of dismissing the mystical, the melancholy, and the difficult. Songs reveal how softness divulges far more than aggression. It does so because it embraces how equal parts dark and light drive the deepest silences. Commotion from a crowd breaks the spell. It threatens to pull us away from the journey. Clap and you have denied yourself and others, the chance to mentally navigate an interior world.

If all this description sounds overtly lofty, or if Sandoval's outrage appears too self-absorbed, you are unlikely to receive a stamp of admission into the cult of Mazzy Star fandom. Many have sought entry and turned their backs, have washed off the stamp's ink, or have proceeded to hide the evidence. Critics who praised their debut later accused their sound of becoming repetitive, monotonous, and boring. Potential fans who attended their shows found the personalities on stage too alienating. Others who wanted the communal experience of a live concert were shushed from whispering along to the music by devotees. Journalists who craved sound bites and headline-worthy dialogue found unbreakable antagonists.

Because if Mazzy Star were frustrating ghosts on stage, they were demons on the press circuit. Roback and Sandoval frequently responded to interviewers with single words and blank expressions. When they answered a question, they tended to speak in loose, abstract snippets which gave the interviewer nothing. Sometimes they contradicted earlier statements—or even each other. Over time, the media responded with open hostility. In 1996, the editors at *Alternative Press* humorously summarized coverage about the band: "Every Mazzy Star story revolves around the interviewer's frustration with David's and Hope's notorious reticence."[2] Viewed from a neutral position, these doomed efforts to pry information are almost comical if they did not also reveal so much venomous effort from the media to break two guarded personalities.

Maybe it sounds like I am making excuses for a band who approached all public scrutiny with vehement detestation. But the stretches of silence, the soft-spoken yet contradictory remarks to interviewers, and the readiness to withdraw from the limelight were not an act. It was Mazzy Star's approach to writing, recording, and releasing music. While they may have wanted their music to reach listeners, Roback and Sandoval likely did not expect to generate such momentous buzz. Nor did they ever think executives at a major label would bet on their success. That was all an accident. Capitol Records absorbed their contract after their previous independent label, Rough Trade went bankrupt. Pressure from corporate leaders hurried *So Tonight That I Might See* (1993) and *Among My Swan* (1996) to shelves. In a curious twist, the major label saved the band from cult obscurity.

INTRODUCTION

Executives pushed "Fade into You" onto the public, they forced the band to create music videos, and they demanded live performances. Not that it fazed Mazzy Star. Presented with an opportunity for fame and momentum, Roback and Sandoval ran off to London, or Norway, or Berkeley to lay low and avoid further touring. Pressed for a response to their sudden success, Roback and Sandoval reacted with characteristic indifference. The one sign of their enthusiasm? Endless appeals for Capitol Records to release them from their contract. Freedom from their overlords came with fan anticipation. What would the band do when fully in control? What experiments would we be privy to hear? Mazzy Star greeted every anxious fan with seventeen years of silence.

The reverence, and annoyance, produced by their reclusion has created a problem. It is often *the* defining quality highlighted to understand their music. Look up profiles about Mazzy Star, watch online videos about the group, and read nostalgia piece after nostalgia piece. David Roback and Hope Sandoval suffer from the introvert's curse. Reticence meant they became cyphers of not what they were but what many people wanted.

This fragment of the curse especially plagued Hope Sandoval. Being female means people project their fantasies. The less Sandoval gave, the more the public dreamt. Such tendencies explain why images of Sandoval circulate so easily on TikTok and Instagram. Intrigue and shyness provide an icon who is not dragged down by the weight of dated opinion. Then there is the physical beauty. Sandoval looks like she sounds: haunting and ethereal. Reader, go online, find a video, and read a comment board. Post after post discusses her physical appearance. It is enough to make you remember why the singer preferred to remain unlit on stage. Roback is not wholly unaffected. Forgotten in recent overt focus on Sandoval is that Roback's guitar playing is a central character in Mazzy Star's music. More than that, it's a co-narrator, feeding off Sandoval's singing, bouncing off it, and trading ideas. In other words, it is equally responsible for the dreamy atmosphere.

The goal of this book is to challenge the trend of superficial responses to Mazzy Star in order to recover the surreal power within their sound. I aim to highlight the mysticism of Sandoval and Roback's songwriting, not to strip their dynamic and output of its mysterious magic, but to navigate and correct the inconsistent stories floating around. Though other musicians—Keith Mitchell, Suki Ewers, Jill Emery, and more—fulfilled various roles in the group, Roback and Sandoval are the band's constant stars. In learning more about the forces that drove these two together, and that carried them from one band to the next, and one album to the next, we will find that there is also far more to their music than mood and dreamscape. This book's opening chapter explores the legacy of their hit "Fade into You" and how it bares their earliest influences. Chapters 2 and 3 trace Roback and Sandoval's upbringing and early ventures into artmaking. Chapter 4 explores their unusual and unlikely rise to mainstream success, the legacy of a band who are the epitome of the Sad Girl style, and the essence of artistry over commercialism. Along the way, the reader will discover that within Mazzy Star, there are traces of a Los Angeles overwhelmed by fantasy and violence, hopeful protests and tragic defeats; there are the sounds of the Paisley Underground; there are strains and allusions of surrealism, Chicano politics, Mexican iconography, and a blend of American blues and psychedelic rock.

So Tonight That I Might See is Mazzy Star's defining work. Many of its songs emerged in uncertain moments, when the band members were uncertain of their future. Others came out of necessity. Though they were guarded to the press, the album itself is a testament to the importance of the personal and to those moments when one does need to open up to others. It is the album in which Roback and Sandoval embraced melancholy yet also opened themselves to the possibility of a brighter future. In the process, they offered catharsis to those unafraid to explore a spectrum of emotions. They were back home in Los Angeles when they recorded it, and while there, they wondered how their hometown defined who they became and what would become of the city in the future—whether it would stay open or close itself off to offbeat dreamers. Never again were Roback and Sandoval so vulnerable.

To better understand *So Tonight That I Might See*—to better understand Mazzy Star's Hope Sandoval and David Roback—do not be afraid to drift off from reality. Escape the comfort of noise and distraction. We will need to embrace silence. We will need to learn to listen.

Fade into You

"I'm not a surrealist. I just paint what I see."—Frida Kahlo

I

The embrace of the American Southwest as a surreal landscape is a familiar trope for Mexican artists to draw upon. From Raul Guerrero's painting *Sonoran Desert—Flora, Fauna, Artifacts* and its evocation of the desert setting as a nexus where a hellish colonial present is forever at odds with the region's Indigenous pasts; to the landscape as a site of personal reflection in Alejandro G. Iñárritu's *Bardo, False Chronicle of a Handful of Truths* and a site of emotional torment in the filmmaker's *Babel*; to the place where modernization collapses in Valeria Luiselli's novel *Lost Children Archive*; to the location where a people's identity becomes shattered by a human-invented border as depicted by sculptor Rafael Lozano Hemmer's *Border Tuner*; to the final step in the journey toward citizenship in Los Lobos' immigrant anthem "The Road to Gilda Bend"; to an area to connect with ancestry and nature in Rudolfo Anaya's *Bless*

Me, Ultima; to an arena of heartbreak in Santana's "Written in Sand" and Selena Gomez's "A Year Without Rain" (also recorded as "Un Año Sin Lluvia")—the American Southwest to the Mexican thinker is a totem of difficult living and thriving despite the circumstances. That somehow, despite it being so inhospitable, a culture, mythology, ambition, and dreams pervade the landscape. The reality of the region becomes intertwined with the strangeness of the fables and stories it produces.

Mazzy Star are a band who recreate this intersection, who wish to show how the world is fragmented, and how real life is best understood in the abstract. It is no surprise that in their most accessible album *So Tonight That I Might See*, Hope Sandoval and David Roback invite listeners to journey with them through the American Southwest. Along the way, they show you that life and dreams are not so far apart. They show you a reality that is deeper and stranger than initially suspected. They present to you a surrealism.

II

What is surrealism? To its European practitioners of the 1920s, surrealism aimed to uncover the unconscious and reveal repressed sexual and psychological forces which move humanity. André Breton, writer of the *Surrealist Manifesto*, offers as clear a definition as any when he states that surrealism is "Psychic automatism in its pure state, by which one proposes to express—verbally, by means of the written word, or in any other manner—the actual functioning of thought. Dictated by the thought, in the absence of any control exercised by reason, exempt from any aesthetic or moral concern."[1] At the risk of oversimplifying an artistic movement filled with artists of different genders, various nationalities, and political beliefs, surrealism is a tradition which rejects rational modes of thought because its practitioners believe the mind and human action do not always work through cogent means. Think of Salvador Dalí's *Persistence of Memory* and its melting clocks. Think of René Magritte's *The Son of Man*, which features a man in a black overcoat whose face is obscured by a green apple. Or think of Magritte's *The Treachery of Images*, which confuses and antagonizes spectators with the claim "ceci n'est pas une pipe" written underneath an image of a pipe. Artwork from this mold often aims to literally recreate what a dream feels like, or what (non)logic a nightmare contains. If one could approximate the unconscious, the surrealists supposed they could represent a vision of individuality that cracked the barriers of human politeness and dishonesty. Emotion in art required unmasking the privileged structures of reason society imposed on them.

Surrealism in its European context was shocking, an affront to colonial societies which clung to rationality in the pursuit of power over other people. The new embrace of dream-worlds was far less novel to the Indigenous and Mexican artists the Europeans encountered in their travels. In one hilarious (and apocryphal) story, Salvador Dalí journeyed to Mexico, only to cut his visit short and promise to never return due to a personal frustration. He claimed, "I can't stand to be in a country more surrealist than my paintings."[2] Mexican culture is fantastical. The country and its art blend its precolonial past with a present view of the world that is open to color, nature and its diversity, and unrestricted emotion. Other surrealists, while less dramatic than Dalí, journeyed toward the American Southwest and encountered qualities in the Mexican American and Indigenous (especially Navajo, Zuni, Hopi) artwork which already reflected their aspirations to depict the irrational side of human life. In short, these cultures had no masks to shed, no rational structures of thought to disavow. Artists like Frida Kahlo had no need to discover a world of dreams because this world was already part of their reality. They told a different story. The subconscious isn't strange. The world we are living in is strange. It is already surreal—we need only look. We need only remember to *see*.

Mazzy Star fuses the two traditions. It is no mere accident that Kevin Kerslake's official music video for "Fade into You" opens with Hope Sandoval opening her eyes. Illuminated by a blue-tone light, they are all that is visible. Shadows cover the rest of her face. Slowly, the shot dissolves until we see the world from her perspective. Everything is lit by the sun. But the light also causes any motion and action to drag. We are in the passenger seat of a car, watching Roback's hands turn the wheel. As we discover from here on, the band moves along the road, traversing the Mojave Desert, and taking in an image of the landscape that feels off. An inordinate amount of time is spent focused on what can survive this landscape. Shots linger on the mechanical (a train and its tracks) and the natural (a tall Joshua tree) and the spaces where these aspects intersect (crows on electric wires). Buildings are dilapidated. The old train station is falling apart. But there is no violence. The world simply adjusts. Crows linger and fly off from utility pole wires. The music plays over all these images. "Fade into You," a song which speaks to abstract dichotomies—"I look to you, and I see nothing"—plays.[3] The song and the video act as an invitation to reevaluate how we perceive the world. Hope's final refrain is thus a challenge: "... it's strange you never knew..."[4] She doesn't give us what we don't know. But the clue is there in the song and video. It's strange we never knew to slow down and to notice what so many other artists have located in the desert—the surreal.

III

For their sophomore album, Mazzy Star were dragged into the desert sunlight. Nowhere is this more noticeable than in the produced publicity around "Fade Into You." The band's lead single off the album was originally released in 1993—in the appropriate month of October. An earlier and less-seen music video, directed by Merlyn Rosenberg, featured the band in shaded blue-gray tones, scarcely visible, and intercut with a first-person camera leading viewers through an unnamed interior that might as well be the haunted house of a teenager's gothic dreams. Lead singer Hope Sandoval is kept at a distance. She is left in a hazy shadow. She hides herself with her long brunette hair. True to the spirit of the band's gloomy and removed aesthetic, this original music video was nonetheless not the sort of work to generate airplay on MTV.

The record executives at Capitol demanded the haunted house open its windows. They wanted people to see the band; they wanted people to *see* Hope Sandoval. Within months, a second music video debuted on MTV which rendered the band more visible. For a group that kept the stage lights off, whose singer was likely to turn her back to the audience to avoid the sight of strangers, and whose guitarist believed in music which urged one to withdraw and look inward, the new footage must have felt vulnerable. In subsequent interviews about live performance and music videos, Sandoval admitted audience expectations for excitement and spectacle left her uncomfortable.[5]

It would be tempting to write off this second video. To dismiss it as uncharacteristic, a forced and hurried visual experiment from a band who disliked such an intense visual spotlight. After all, their subsequent visual output is almost nonexistent. Surely that simple fact is revealing? Fans might also feel inclined to scoff at the video for what Quinn Moreland describes as the obvious "undertext of a decision to push a female frontperson further into the spotlight [because] beauty (or, more cynically, sex) sells."[6] Such censure—though fair—is too simple. To make the video, the band turned to Kevin Kerslake, a familiar collaborator. His direction for their first album's "Halah" colors Sandoval and Roback in a distinct palette, as if technicolor had been dripped with acid. Kerslake's return brought the same complimentary and experimental touch. Without the veneer of abstract color or absolute darkness, the song and video offer themselves up as an open gateway into the surreal iconography which drives the band's music.

Of course, openness does not necessarily equate to being explicable. "Fade into You" begins with a guitar strumming. Nine seconds pass before the slide guitar enters to perform the melody. It's a magical moment. Without that start, the song would not feel right. The slide guitar fades into the background as Sandoval sings. It's a conscious and unconscious catharsis, a presence the song falls back upon. All the adjectives that could further describe the melody, all the words that try to explain Sandoval's soft singing, all the particulars about the key signature, fail to accurately convey the accumulating ethereal effect. It's not a challenge to understand why the song has endured. It is difficult to wonder why it is so effective. One could state how the song shares a chord progression with Bob Dylan's "Knocking On Heaven's Door." Both tunes speak to a fleetingness about human existence. Yet Dylan's rejection of violence for the possibility of a Christian afterlife suggests story and movement. "Fade into You" lacks this linear momentum. It contains a chorus; however, the song's tempo never changes and there is no direct momentum. "Fade into You" does not even end. The volume simply diminishes. To put it another way, the song closes with a self-reflexive gesture. It literally fades out.

Today, "Fade into You" is everywhere. It is by far Mazzy Star's most well-known song. An unscientific eye and ear test suggests it haunts far too many uploads of autumn landscapes. The song soundtracks thousands of "get dressed with me" videos. It is the background to many relationship announcements and many more confessions about first loves, first broken hearts, and nostalgia for adolescence.

There are no signs this usage will slow. Not bad for a song written in a single day.[7] With each passing year, an eclectic bunch of musicians cover the song. At the time of writing, Miley Cyrus, Paolo Nutini, Ben Harper, American Football, Mallrat, Inhaler, Muzz, Kelly Clarkson, J. Mascis of Dinosaur Jr. with Fred Armisen, and Valerie June have recently covered the song. With rare exception, few performers have altered the song's lyrics, its tempo, or its style. Though these artists retain so many of the song's core elements, none quite succeed. However much I like some of these performers, no one quite captures the power within the track. No one quite melds Roback's instrumentation with Sandoval's warm melancholic delivery.

In addition to its online omnipresence, it survives as the go-to song to soundtrack heartbreak and doomed love. *Gilmore Girls*, *Daria*, *3 Body Problem*, *CSI*, *Dopesick*, *Yellowjackets*, *Desperate Housewives*, *American Honey*, *Riverdale*, *Starship Troopers*, and countless other television shows and films have used it to that effect. No wonder it was once voted by *Vulture* as the most overused song in film and television![8] Music supervisors need to convince audiences that their characters are romantically misunderstood? To summon nostalgia for an innocent love? To arouse sadness? Well, "Fade into You" is the permanent cheat code.

The song conjures romance. This interpretation is rarely deliberated upon. Part of this is the fault of the marketers at Capitol Records who pushed the track upon teenagers as make-out music. It's not a wrong interpretation—if there is ever such a thing. Though these romantic readings have tended to confuse me. The song flirts with an unnamed partner. Sandoval lingers on the word "nothing" to describe this figure, and the more she looks, the more she finds someone whose eyes contain "colors" with "what's not there."[9] In the blankness, the singer becomes so consumed with an encroaching night, loneliness at the end of the evening, and the simultaneous thrill and comfort that comes from being alone. I suppose I have trouble with the sole emphasis on romantic longing because the song contains a warning wrapped in melancholy for the listener. Nearly every line uses the second person. "You" are called forward into the action, into the emotion, and into the eerie illustrations of Sandoval's lyrics. Until the album's final titular song, nowhere else does this gesture appear on the album. For a band famously media-averse, and who "visualized [their music] being played late at night ... something that happens around midnight in a darkened room," the recurrent use of the second-person "you" is bold and perplexing.[10] The soft, near-whisper singing adds an urgency to quiet down. The breaking of the fourth wall calls us in. In fact, it pulls us into Mazzy Star's world.

IV

Hope Sandoval was born on June 24, 1966, in East Los Angeles. That same year, the historian Susan M. Anderson argues, represents the zenith of surrealist activity and interest in the art style across Southern California.[11] If we judge the criteria of artistic output and public attention on the basis of a museum exhibit and highbrow magazine, then Anderson has a solid claim to make. The then-Los Angeles-based magazine *Artforum* devoted a whole issue to surrealism in the region, and New York's Museum of Modern Art organized a René Magritte retrospective in Pasadena.

From the 1930s to 1950s, surrealists descended on Los Angeles to infect the arts. Salvador Dalí, Max Ernst, Igor Stravinsky, Dorothea Tanning all spent substantial time in the city. Some, like Man Ray, made it their permanent home. The rising tide of war, fascism, and authoritarian rule across Europe had inspired many to flee the continent. Southern California was an especially attractive destination. There was the climate. There was also a landscape which contained a desert, a beach, and a mountainside all within a day's drive. Then there was LA, the City of Angels, which simultaneously felt like the edge of the earth and the center of it. The city and its people were obsessed with the new. Buildings were rarely a century old. Cars displaced people at all turns. Movie stars emerged to absorb the imagination and alter people's fantasies. As Man Ray put it, "There was more Surrealism rampant in Hollywood than all the Surrealists could invent in a lifetime."[12] Money, also, was key. The city offered a glut of potential financiers who acquired wealth due to the booming oil and entertainment industries. These same people, many of these artists hoped, could help them succeed in film and television.

The surrealists believed they could bend mainstream entertainment to their vision. Show business, however, proved unconquerable as each industry extracted all it could from the surrealists while simultaneously dismissing their radical, political, and social ambitions. It sanitized the overt challenges to sexual and personal expression. The most famous marriage of commercial commerce and surreal art comes in Hitchcock's 1945 film *Spellbound*, which features a dream sequence designed by Salvador Dalí. While Dalí's original plan was edited down due to expense and technical complications—and likely potential censorship—the faceless figures, the buildings which look to be dissolving into water, and eerie transformations of everyday objects have influenced countless visuals. Even if they could not get their films made, executives used the artists for publicity. Man Ray became an art director and on-set photographer, capturing stars like Ava Gardner in costume. Elsewhere, Disney made it a point to recruit European expats familiar with surrealism for their animated films. This brief recapitulation initially suggests a doomed perspective about the ability of surrealism to survive Tinseltown. But surrealism is a strange force. It resurfaced elsewhere to great cultural effect.

There are two noteworthy counters to Anderson's argument that surrealism in Los Angeles peaked in 1966. First is the city itself. Los Angeles was built on the foundation of a Hispanic culture which clung to its Indigenous pasts. The city and its industries absorbed this influence. It would be accurate to say that in these Hispanic corners of the city, surrealism never died. It never was brought over. It existed from the start. What we call surreal, or what details we can now add as part of the movement and genre, long played a role in the city's existence. And second, around the time the old masters of the surreal entered their twilight years, surrealism resurfaced in the moods and sounds of psychedelic rock. Raised on surrealism via cheap paperbacks, odd bits in films, and their city of LA, musicians became interested in unpacking the kaleidoscope of the human mind. Both rebuttals emerge from Anderson's failure to recognize the artistic value within the mainstream—what has sometimes been called lowbrow. Art created for the common person and art which emerges from a common culture are crucial. Anderson, in short, is too focused on thinking about surrealism as a high art tradition carried on by artists who get media coverage and exhibitions.

LA is surrealism incarnate. Three hundred days of annual sunshine tend to confuse the mind. Days bleed together. Relentless warmth muddles any sense of time. It is a town where an industry devoted to make-believe drives the economy. Ignore the moguls and the frustrated, scared executives, and look at the backlot. Actors in costumes representing different periods and genres cross paths. Such odd juxtapositions would not look out of place in a Leonora Carrington sketch. The same industry flocked to the area for its sunny climate. Yet, the industry fakes the weather. When the temperature pushes a hundred, crews work to ensure the snow looks real. Noirs set in the area are almost always pouring rain, though the city scarcely averages more than a month of rain a year. Many inaccurately believe, because of these films, that LA exists at the edge of an ocean and at the edge of the desert. It's a place of extreme ends. LA as dream and nightmare has most benefited the transplants. Non-Angelenos flock to neighborhoods full of ambitious like-minded others in the hopes of joining or embracing the paradoxical facades the entertainment industry upholds. They drive in their cars and ignore those few who walk, those pedestrians who are willing to see LA from the perspective of fragile ground.

Get away from the glitzy industry, and one encounters far more degrees of the surreal. Films about the city often fail to accurately show LA's multicultural population. Worse, is that popular portrayals of LA ignore the city's significant Hispanic presence. It is a curious tendency when we remember that this population built this city long before the US stole the Southwest. Not far from Downtown Los Angeles, one encounters El Pueblo de Los Ángeles, an area with origins back to the Spanish. But the Indigenous, Mexican, US, and Spanish cultures clash as one travels through Olvera Street. Walk along the street and you will find vendors who sell wares of the sort that likely frustrated and terrified Dalí. Skeletons which grin, equipment for altars which celebrate the dead, folk art that anthropomorphizes nature, puppets devoted to the Mother Mary and non-Christian figures, and toys which parody and celebrate contemporary interests are all available. It is a sample of a larger Mexican culture.

Growing up in East Los Angeles, an area where over four-fifths of the population claims Hispanic heritage, it is hard to fathom Hope Sandoval never having visited. It is harder to fathom these cultural signifiers never having played an influence. On a recent trip to the market on Olvera Street, I found a yellow-colored stand and held up trinket after trinket. Eventually, something caught my eye. Placed in a crowded corner was a hand-painted Milagro. For those who do not know, Milagro means "miracle." It is a charm in the Southwest and Latin American world with a variety of meanings and purposes. People frequently hold onto these charms to pray and seek blessings. The particular Milagro in my palm was red and heart-shaped. It weighed little. Over the red paint were tiny metal fragments. A few crosses and a few human faces. Not much detail was etched onto these objects except for the same lifted smile on each face. Looking back on this Milagro, I cannot help but recall a wonderfully eerie moment from "Fade into You." Sandoval sings to you. She describes the way a smile can cover a truth, the way a smile can "cover your heart."[13]

In the late 1960s, musicians from the West Coast embraced surrealism to elevate rock music into the category of serious art. In addition, the rise of psychedelic drugs like LSD offered artists a perceived gateway to alternative ways of thinking, to challenging their perceptions, and to privileging the irrational sides of their minds. Is that not also what the surrealists aspired to do? The popularization of hallucinogens and rabid journalists eager to demarcate the music as revolutionary—as psychedelic or acid rock— are the major reasons we do not immediately refer to the output of this era as surrealist. Yet, West Coast bands were interested in this tradition and in adding to it. Jimi Hendrix sought to blend his dreams with his favorite science fiction in "Purple Haze." The song's first lines capture the experience of mania, of a loose mind causing the body to act on impulse. In 1968's *Head*, a musical film co-written by Jack Nicholson, the Monkees deconstructed their corporate-created image by breaking their fourth wall in a series of vignettes that feel better suited to a Luis Buñuel production. For their 1967 album *Smiley Smile*, The Beach Boys collaborated with Frank

J. Holmes to create a cover inspired by Henri Rousseau's appropriately titled *The Dream*. On their aptly named *Surrealistic Pillow*, Jefferson Airplane shared their devotion to the surreal in a song entitled "White Rabbit." The track summarizes surrealism's patron saint Alice from the Lewis Carroll novels as she ingests pills, takes mushrooms, and describes the death of logic.

To David Roback and Hope Sandoval, the most significant rock surrealists were The Doors and Love. It is not a coincidence that both acts formed in Los Angeles, and that both were led by frontmen who spent their childhoods in the city. A few short years after The Mamas & the Papas sang about moving to Los Angeles for warmth and safety on "California Dreamin'," Jim Morrison and Arthur Lee wrote records to warn everyone that sunshine brings shadows. It is important to remember that the Tate-LaBianca murders committed by members of the Manson Family occurred in the late summer of 1969. Given that Roback was eleven when this occurred, The Doors and Love likely felt closer to capturing the violent undercurrent of his hometown. Jim Morrison, who especially loved Antonin Artaud, an artist whose films and plays were some of the earliest in the surrealist scene, told of the murkiness obscured by the city's sunshine. On "Twentieth Century Fox," Morrison exposes the city's most famous industry by linking a movie studio's name to predatory misogyny. "Break on Through (to the Other Side)" is a call to arms to reach alternate forms of consciousness. Mazzy Star alter Morrison's famous claims from this track on their first album's "Ghost Highway."[14] Sandoval speaks to the ghost, that phantom on the other side of this life, and declares to it, "your eyes are an island, and I'll hold you forever."[15] An obsession with sight, with the way what we see can trick us, is already present. So is the surreal want to bridge life with death. And whereas the Doors' mysterious track "The End" culminates in a lengthy poem in which the reality uncovered by surrealism is apocalyptic, Roback and Sandoval find a more optimistic angle to the world as surreal. Look outside, Sandoval suggests in their second album's titular finale, and notice "sunshine on a rainy day."[16]

While traces of Jim Morrison pop up in Hope Sandoval's lyrics, it should be stressed that the Doors and Love were, arguably, more important to David Roback. Born on April 4, 1958, and raised in Brentwood, an area in the westernmost section of Los Angeles, Roback had two hobbies at a young age: history and psychiatry.[17] Fusing these disciplines, Roback longed to understand how personal and social histories informed people's perceptions. He psychoanalyzed neighbors and friends, trying to figure out why people became aggressive and how to treat the mind to avoid unhealthy obsessions. It isn't hard to believe a kid who practiced Freudian psychoanalysis would become a social pariah in his neighborhood. But, in his view, it was a good thing. Roback embraced his outsider status. Observing others and their behaviors created opportunities for self-reflection. Why did he feel so different? Why did he not want to snap to anger? Why was he so excited to sit alone and detach himself from the neighborhood?

When Roback discovered the Doors and Love, he believed these were kindred spirits. Each band blended his two interests into an art which discussed feelings about life in LA that he struggled to articulate. That they were active and writing songs on the other side of town, performing in venues at the other end of a freeway, and living within a reasonable distance had a profound effect on him. Recalling the sensation, David Roback commented, "I just thought they were speaking from a world I really wanted to be part of."[18] In a public remembrance, Susanna Hoffs, Roback's childhood friend, recurring bandmate, and eventual lead singer of The Bangles, clarifies what this world contained. Hoffs describes Roback's want for the "darkly mysterious" and to create music which could be "the light that attracted the dark."[19] However distant the late 1960s became, Roback constantly returned to The Doors and Love for inspiration, for finding ways to balance beauty and ugliness.

Compared to The Doors, Love's influence on Mazzy Star is understated. More upfront than any Mazzy Star number, Love crafted tracks which demand that you turn the stereo up. Fusing mariachi, classical orchestra, jazz, and folk, Love's brand of psychedelic rock remains poppy, energetic, and propulsive. At least until you look at the lyrics and songwriter. Love's primary songwriter was Arthur Lee, a Black man who embodied the contradictions of Los Angeles. Usually coy about what he learned and appropriated from his forebears, Roback gushed about his fandom.[20] Prior to recording *So Tonight That I Might See*, the two met and exchanged tunes. It is a curious pairing of minds. One wonders what they discussed and what they thought about one another. Unfortunately, their conversation has gone to their graves.

The self-declared "first Black hippie" had a reputation for being anything but a calm, peace-loving individual.[21]

Management, Lee's bandmates, and countless others have passed on stories on in which Lee's generosity was outmatched by shocking behaviors of protopunk rage.[22] Lee led the multiracial band Love across his hometown, where they earned a reputation for their sloppy yet thrilling rock club concerts on the Sunset Strip. They recorded their landmark 1967 album *Forever Changes* at The Castle, a dilapidated mansion rumored to have once housed Bela Lugosi. By withdrawing into a distant side of Los Angeles, Lee also disavowed the public's demands and wants of its rock stars. Distance freed him to experiment with how music could reveal the seediness hidden by the expressed optimism of the hippie movement. As Andrew Hultkrans notes, Arthur Lee kept some distance from the flower power movement because he believed it was insufficient and hypocritical as a means to address the problems of poverty or racial tension that he witnessed as a Black man.[23] The 1960s counterculture had changed people's behaviors and attitudes, but it didn't change them fast enough. Lee struggled to expand Love's popularity due to racial hostility in much of the United States that limited where the band toured.[24] While others centered LA as a place of freedom and collective protests, Lee recognized racial and economic segregation. He watched his childhood neighborhood burn down during the Watts Riots of 1965.

Love was made possible because of LA's multicultural population and its 1960s role as a center in the thought that popular culture from the coast could inspire and drive positive change across the world. Tragically, the band was also confined by it. Lee channels this paradoxical nature best on

Forever Changes' "The Red Telephone" and "andmoreagain." In "The Red Telephone," Lee juxtaposes folksy guitar with the morbid claims of watching people die.[25] Over romantic and sweeping orchestral strings on "andmoreagain," Lee delivers a wicked set of poetic lines which recall Sandoval's own twisted phrasings on "Fade into You." As the music crescendos into a warm and comforting phrase, Lee falls into pessimistic worry.[26] Adopting a tone reminiscent of Burt Bacharach, the music seems to almost want to cover the melancholia within the vocals. Until it can't. The strings strike. They sound like his heartbeat. Lee senses both and describes it through the onomatopoeia of "thrum-pum-pum-pum."[27] The unconscious has risen to the surface. It will not go away. Overall, Love is a soundtrack for the failed promises of the 1960s. It reminds us how quickly dreams can descend into nightmares.

The Doors and Love are hardly the only influences on Mazzy Star, but to David Roback, they provided a template for how music might revel in a strange state: that fleeting instance between pleasure and melancholy, and between the rational and irrational. If the Doors preached unreality by capturing the hazy quality of too many alcoholic drinks, emerging from a bar into the twilight, and recreating the ugliness that coincides with lust, they did so boorishly. Jim Morrison's voice booms. He sounds dangerous. The organ rises to the ominous mood. The other instruments come individually alive so you can almost pick out each one. Conversely, Arthur Lee's crooning is so soft it comes across as sweet. Lee's voice matches the instrumental melody. There are moments when music and singer are one, and many when the former overwhelms the latter. Without careful attention, Lee's singing gets lost. When it comes to creating his sound, Roback draws on the two singers. But Roback did not have a voice; he had a guitar. At times he had a piano. On "Mary of Silence," Roback pulls a Morrison. As the singer tracks a descent into madness, the guitar takes over, replicating a restless state of mental terror. On "Five String Serenade"—an Arthur Lee cover—Roback replicates Lee's singing on the original track even as Sandoval transforms the melody from a ballad of heartwarming commitment to despondent devotion.

For a child obsessed with history, Roback never found a problem in channeling these ghosts as stylistic models. After their first album's release, Roback confessed that all artists are part of a larger tradition. With that creed comes a freedom to mine the past to better define the present.[28] At the same time, Roback was not interested in merely recreating history or covering it in Mazzy Star. The other key element here is his deep interest in psychiatry. As thoughtful as Morrison and Lee were about their world and city, they were not always self-reflective. Roback sought for his music to wrestle with the mind. But it was not enough to reveal his own thoughts and feelings. He wanted his guitar to motivate others to examine their unconscious. Oscillating from soft to coarse, from the sweet to the booming, Roback achieved his sound by drawing on Lee and Morrison and filtering these tones through a haze. It's impossible not to notice it, even when Hope Sandoval sings. Whether it's the simple chords strummed on an acoustic, the striking tone from the slide guitar, or the ringing distortion of an electric instrument,

Roback's guitar tone hums. It carries us through our abstract emotions. Whatever the song, the sound disarms like the sudden dark. It causes us to see reality like a dream. It urges us to look inward. It urges us to imagine.

VI

People tend to interpret "Fade into You" as romantic, yet few ever consider the simple philia love of two people who have found companionship, not as sexual or romantic partners, but as friends who can comfortably bare their souls to one another. Roback and Sandoval embraced the rare challenge of understanding history and psychiatry about each other and about their city. On "Fade into You," when Sandoval sings that chorus, she is singing it to us, and she also sings it to Roback. This devotion is made clear in the music video. As Sandoval and Roback journey through the desert, we are privy to Sandoval's fantasy of being on stage in near darkness. It is especially telling that as the scenes dissolve between the two worlds, Roback enters the spotlight. "Fade into You" is frequently thought to be about how we give ourselves to another at the risk of losing who we are. But if we accept that Sandoval and Roback are one, that they are Mazzy Star, then it's not so negatively sacrificial. It's about someone surrendering their emotional guard. A terrifying thing to do. Toward the video's end, Roback continues driving. Sandoval seems to lean over the front seat. Her arms are draped in a loose fashion, and her hands are softly wrapped. Next to her is Roback's arm. There is comfort in being together. There is comfort wherever life takes someone. It's a strange part of life. As Sandoval reminds us in her singing, it's a truth so many don't realize. It's "strange you never knew . . ."[29]

The understated genius of Mazzy Star is that they convey the belief that the surreal is not limited to the confusion within our unconscious minds, and that instead what we should deem surreal is the spark which occurs so often in our connection to others. It's the bizarre want to connect with others. It's the bizarre want to be left alone. Surreal is the ability to understand what another person feels. Surreal is the privilege to access another's thoughts. That Roback and Sandoval would hint at such a philosophy is powerful. These are two quiet introverts whose melancholy is mistaken for sadness. But here they are, presenting the reverse: community and imagination. Surreal is to give up being alone and to let yourself become part of another's life. To sit and embrace another because that's what human beings should do. "Fade into You" is a soft song packed with detail and emotion meant to carry your imagination. It is easy to miss the lesson. But as the old maxim goes: when someone shy speaks up, it's best to pay attention.

Bells Ring

I

Mazzy Star is seldom, if ever, considered in the context or tradition of Chicano music. Such an oversight is surprising when we consider that lead singer Hope Sandoval has cited Spanish music as an influence on her singing and songwriting, that she grew up in a Mexican American household, that she spent her formative years in the predominantly Hispanic East Los Angeles, and that teenage friend and Chicana Sylvia Gomez played an influential role in Sandoval's songwriting. Equally remarkable is that Mazzy Star's rise coincided with a significant breakthrough of Latine-fronted media in US popular culture.

Part of the reason for Mazzy Star's omission in these discussions about Chicano soundscapes lies in the group's intense adversity to the media. Hope Sandoval rarely elaborated on her background or its place in her music—nor was or is she required to do so. In addition, she did not fit the public image of what a female Mexican American singer looked or sang like. She was not Linda Ronstadt, who spoke openly about her ancestry and embraced her roots in an album devoted to Mariachi. She was not Joan Baez, who discussed how racial epithets about her and her Mexican father informed her social activism. She was not Selena Quintanilla, who fused Spanish traditionalism with an interest in Madonna. There is also the fact that, unlike Los Lobos, Mazzy Star included David Roback, a white guitarist whom early critics often zeroed in on as the creative force within the band. There is also a rather simple truth. The band's music embraces non-Latine traditions proudly by drawing on country music, the blues, and early Rolling Stones.

However, the story of Hope Sandoval and Mazzy Star should not be ignored by the Latine community. Sandoval's breakthrough as an artist parallels the intertwined political advancement and cultural popularity of Chicano movements in the latter half of the twentieth century. This narrative is long overdue. One might as well start with the pioneering rock forefather Ritchie Valens. Born on May 13, 1941, the Mexican American Valens was the child of migrant laborers who left the agricultural fields in pursuit of success in LA's northwest San Fernando Valley. At his family's encouragement, Valens taught himself guitar, blending the mariachi and flamenco music of his relatives with the rhythm and blues he heard on the radio.[1] He was still a high schooler when his local performances garnered comparisons to Little Richard and earned him a deal with Del-Fi Records. Talent carried him only so far. He shortened his surname from Valenzuela to Valens to counter discrimination. DJs of the era would not play a Chicano's songs.[2] Now comes the mystical part you probably know. Valens's star was on the rise. He had released four chart-making songs and was on pace to rival many of his idols. Then, at just seventeen years old, he climbed with Buddy Holly and the Big Bopper into a plane during a snowstorm. Music would evolve without him.

Valens's story haunts all Chicanos who pursue music because it blends cautious tragedy with aspirational genius. Because it reminds us of a harsh truth: death is indifferent to a dreamer. Here is a kid who escaped the conditions of urban destitution to celebrate a marginalized culture. On the unforgettable "La Bamba," Valens updated a folk song from Mexico with an electric guitar and got millions of white Americans to dance and sing to a song in Spanish.[3] It's not without irony that Valens, like many non-first-generation Mexican Americans, did not speak much of the language.[4] Nonetheless, we should not understate the shock of such an achievement. Four years before "La Bamba's" release, the US government embarked on "Operation Wetback," a nationwide initiative which aimed to forcibly deport Mexican migrants.[5] Through mass raids and sweeps, designated officials were tasked with quickly and aggressively deporting illegal residents in mass numbers. The result was that a significant number of those removed were documented or legal citizens.[6] Coverage of the event led to an outcry from the Mexican American public. Not that it did much to reduce targeted attacks by authority figures and institutions. One of the ugliest assaults occurred in LA on May 5, 1959, when police officers violently evicted residents from the Chavez Ravine neighborhood. After a decade of tense opposition, the largely Mexican American neighborhood watched crews raze their homes and remodel the land for the eventual building of Dodger Stadium.[7]

That "La Bamba" could become a crossover hit despite ongoing racial oppression is a testament to Valens's talent and to the notion that music can cross cultural divides. In doing so, it became the template for generations of Latine rock singers who aimed to capture English-speaking audiences. It also ushered in a curse. Success for the Latine musician in the United States meant embracing Spanish. If the singer did not speak or sing in Spanish, then the music should sound Spanish—whatever that may mean. Audiences expected it. Audiences craved it. In today's parlance, audiences believed Latine and Chicano music should represent said community. To pull away from the identity, to resist its stereotype, risks upsetting one's own community, and risks dispelling the interest of white audiences.

Chicano musicians face a choice. As Valens did when he sang "La Bamba," one could embrace their identity. Or, as Valens did when he forfeited his original last name, one could hide from it. Let's put it another way: to assimilate or not? Bold demonstrations of culture are not inherently bad. Bands like Thee Midniters refused to denounce their Mexican heritage. After finding some success with a "Land of a 1000 Dances," they fought for cultural empowerment and a united front in 1967's "Chicano Power." They recreated the thrill of cruising across East LA in "Whittier Boulevard." On "The Ballad of Cesar Chavez," they covered the battles of the titular activist with a corrido vernacular that made the details of his strikes accessible to the communities most affected. So what if the approach limited their appeal? Thee

Midniters soundtracked the lives of many Chicanos in East Los Angeles who protested unsafe working conditions, police brutality, poor education, housing segregation, and other racist institutions. Conversely, the members of Question Mark and the Mysterians shied from discussing their background as children of migrant Mexican farmers. When they performed on the variety show *Swingin' Time* in 1966, they dressed in sunglasses and polka dot shirts. Lead singer Rudy Martinez danced like Mick Jagger and adopted an accent like he was a lost Davies brother. Martinez, better known as Question Mark, bristled at efforts to determine his ethnicity.[8] Rejecting the ethnic categorization freed the band to explore varied styles of music. It allowed them to play with their mythology and image.

If this initial decision by the members of Question Mark and the Mysterians to disclaim their heritage seems unbecoming, it is only because it is at odds with the many mass demonstrations of the era. "96 Tears" reached the top of the Billboard Hot 100 in August 1966, several months after Cesar Chavez led a group of striking farm laborers over 250 miles into Sacramento to protest exploitative labor conditions.[9] When "Can't Get Enough of You Baby" made its way onto the charts in the spring of 1967, students across high school and college campuses were beginning to organize around identity. In California, Chicano groups embarked on open protests to condemn the inferior resources of their public schools. Editorials were shared to challenge racist claims that the Chicano was mentally inferior and ill-suited for higher education. Anger swelled until high school students in East LA began to walk out of their classrooms on March 1, 1968, in a call for education reform. Days later, the walkouts bloomed, with some estimating that 20,000 students participated in the protests.[10] It was a formidable display of collective action. Young students demanded better conditions. They demanded the possibility of a better future.

Their effort tragically mirrored the Ritchie Valens story. The promising future was cut short. The dream died. Organizers from the protests met with the educational board in fiery exchanges. The result? None of the demands of the protestors were met.[11] Though greater attention came to predominantly minority-serving institutions, old problems persisted. Schools in East LA remained underfunded. Dropout rates fell but remained astonishingly high.[12] Troubles with the schools led to intensified danger in the surrounding neighborhoods. The rise of Latine-fronted art and community action, which was so full of optimism in the 1960s, turned melancholic, and the neighborhoods which fought for community improvements, watched on as crime, violence, and poverty escalated.

Hope Sandoval was born amid this period of unrest, and she experienced the volatile aftermath. Chicano power was a part of her childhood. However, the power faded and as she approached young adulthood, collective battles for progress were replaced with individualism and territorial squabbles. The pride for the culture turned inward. Gangs formed to claim and protect territories. Opportunity for a united front of diverse Chicanos never had a chance. It was a change she saw mirrored at home when her family fractured.

Ever shy about her familial history, this much is clear. Sandoval's father was a butcher, and her mother worked at a factory which produced potato chips. Both were high school dropouts and had children from previous marriages when they met. When Hope Sandoval was born in 1966, she was the youngest of nine, with one full brother and seven half-siblings. A prominent age gap between her and her other siblings meant she grew up feeling like a child lost among adults.[13] Spanish music flooded their household. Her parents played their favorite Mexican songs over and over.[14] These were songs with sad stories, warm and bright sounds that nevertheless channeled melancholy. The union between her parents did not last, and her father was not often around.

By the age of thirteen, Sandoval's surrounding world rapidly decayed into danger. Gangs and drugs across East LA, in Sandoval's words, made day to day survival "really, really rough."[15] Her laconic description understates the harsh reality. Homicide across Los Angeles almost tripled since the year of the walkouts. Law enforcement listed more than thirty-six gangs on a watchlist around the same time. These numbers represented a sharp increase of more than fifty percent from the start of the 1970s.[16] Efforts to disrupt criminal activity through ongoing surveillance and brutal enforcement of teenagers and suspects led to new gangs which sought to combat police detection with greater violence. These groups rarely struggled to gain new recruits. Declines in manufacturing and the recession in the middle of the 1970s led to a reoccurring unemployment rate above the national average.[17] People of color were especially affected by these changes. With less opportunities for jobs in the formal economy, waves of youths turned to the underground market to fulfill their needs.

For such a shy and observant personality, one wonders if Sandoval felt inclined to join a gang to gain a sense of community. Questions also arise about peer pressure, if any, that may have compelled her to participate in the rapidly growing drug use so commonly done to numb the unforgiving urban poverty. Brief biographies suggest Sandoval mostly avoided direct involvement. Yet, her family members did not escape the temptations of circumstance. In a notable admission about her past to *NME*, Sandoval confessed that an older brother was a recognizable neighborhood presence.[18] His involvement in different gangs kept people on alert. It also prevented others from messing with his family. This fact made her experience in town surreal. As a resident of East LA, she heard firsthand the accounts of those like her brother willing to do whatever it took to survive. Sandoval noticed the various acts of the violence. She could sense the mental injuries afflicting her neighbors. All these dark stories and she was uninvolved, able to wander and observe. Free from so much potential harm, the introverted Sandoval became paradoxically more at ease with the seedier elements of her city. As she described the sensation, "when you're in so close with it, you're more comfortable with it."[19]

The familial luck which erased many consequences of the gangs did not solve all her problems. Education was frustrating and difficult. School left her depressed.[20] Classmates got away with what the adults in her neighborhood did not—bullying and teasing her for her debilitating shyness.[21] Reluctance to talk singled her out to school officials as a problem child. It did not help that the teachers did not know how to motivate Sandoval. When she was an infant, Chicano students marched out of their schools to end classroom biases. For too long, authority figures treated the Chicano as incapable of learning. Yet here she was, over a decade since the walkouts, suffering the very problems those students sought to end. Administrators, because of her behavior and because of their assumptions, placed her in special education classes. The experience convinced her to escape, to get out of the classroom by any means necessary.

On those days she refused to go, she hid in her bedroom, playing a guitar she somehow convinced her parents to buy at thirteen, and listening to the Rolling Stones on repeat. Not the volatile *Exile on Main Street* or the more popular *Sticky Fingers*. She preferred the folksy blues created under original founder Brian Jones to the aggressive rock wrought by the Richards and Jagger partnership.[22] An exception was made for the country-tinge numbers on *Let it Bleed* like "Love in Vain." On some of those days, Sylvia Gomez joined her, and they played along to the records, listening and discussing a mutual favorite called "Goin' Home."[23] Over this eleven-minute track, Jagger's voice bounces along to a honky-tonk guitar, and he describes his readiness to sacrifice a life of travel and worldly pursuit for a woman at home. Initially sweet, the song devolves into a frenetic mess, as if the narrator is falling apart, and the band is held together by the surviving strands maintaining his mental sanity. A theme and description which could also describe many tracks by Mazzy Star.

There are direct echoes most on *So Tonight That I Might See*'s "She's My Baby." Sandoval's vocal technique of dragging out the titular lyric sounds awfully close to Jagger's declaration that he will "see my baby."[24] Yet while

Jagger's narrative succumbs to a misogyny through frequent declarations of possession and a finale which hints toward sexual manipulation, Sandoval flips the script. She describes a person who resist ownership. After this person has gone "home all alone" and admits to fantasies of "goin away" the track's narrator admits that a truth opposite of the title's suggestion.[25] Long before Sandoval and Roback built on their Rolling Stones' influences, the song "Goin' Home" soundtracked more than her bedroom, it soundtracked the start of a vision to become a musician. It was a vision that required Sandoval to turn away from the usual cries of Chicano activism.

II

At the start of the 1980s, Chicano activism and culture faced a curious cultural impasse. Ten years since Carlos Santana brought Spanish-inspired blues to a mass audience on 1970's best-selling *Abraxas*, and five years after War taught the public about East LA cruising culture in 1975's "Low Rider," Latine and Hispanic culture was still too segregated. White musicians borrowed from Latin music to great popular effect while Latine musicians floundered at the periphery. The Clash offered a bold statement about the Nicaraguan Revolution and leftist struggles across Latin America in 1980's *Sandinista*. Travels throughout the region introduced David Byrne of the Talking Heads to a variety of Spanish artists like the Cuban Celia Cruz and Dominican leader in Salsa Johnny Pacheco. As the decade marched on, these white, mostly middle-class, and male musicians commercialized Latine struggle. As much as their music informed a public about important crises around the Latin world, it also exoticized these groups and rendered their problems as removed and distant from American and European listeners. The Pixies' "Vamos" and "Isla de Encanta" are two casualties of this effect. Sung in an accented manner, with a slangy Spanish, the songs become a racial pantomime that reduce the locale of Puerto Rico to a place of white fantasy. "Isla de Encanta" assumes the exiles' fantasy of returning to Puerto Rico because the island, according to Black Francis, is devoid of suffering.

Distance from the immediacy of Latine activism was not just the fault of male rock musicians. Madonna pulled Hispanic culture into pop music on MTV. In 1984's "Borderline" music video, the singer hangs out in an East LA bar where she plays pool and flirts with a Latino man. The grunge aesthetic of this ethnic neighborhood contrasts with her interest for a British photographer who lives in a colorless mansion littered with European art. Hindsight suggests there is something bleakly comical about how the song and video combination compare a white woman's struggle with enamored devotion over her ethnic lover as akin to a border. On her third album, Madonna became more explicit in her admiration for Latin America with 1986's "La Isla Bonita." Embracing Spanish and English, and wearing a black Bolero on the single's cover, Madonna fused cultures and watched as another song of hers soared toward the top of the Billboard Hot 100.[26]

But for all the success and appropriation, the Chicano figure was absent from the mainstream. Representation was missing. Anyone who sought immediate Chicano experiences in the early eighties was doomed to witness mediated artwork. A major exception is Cheech and Chong's "Born in East LA," a 1985 hit that parodied the previous year's "Born in the U.S.A" by Bruce Springsteen. The track describes a Chicano who the police mistake for an undocumented immigrant. The narrator proceeds to describe how he returns to East LA, the one place where he is accepted and where he hopes to never leave. Underneath Cheech Marin's guttural vocals and its satirical spin on racial relations in Reagan's America, is a sad story which suggests the East LA Chicano is a pariah. Beyond the boundaries of their neighborhood, no one will listen, and no one cares.

Is it any wonder that Sandoval demonstrates a disinterest in the public's taste? Her own development as a young Chicana artist coincided with political and cultural indifference to the Chicano community's plights and expressions—except via self-parody and pop appropriation. Such an unwelcoming atmosphere was motivation to remain insular. It is for this reason that the early bedroom years are so important. Friendship with Sylvia Gomez gave Sandoval a safe space to express herself and provided her an ideal model for future creative collaboration. It suggested how conversation with other musicians could open pathways. It also suggested the importance of an audience—preferably a patient one. Some songs were drawn from magic. Compelled by an indeterminable force, an inexplicable intensity would wash over her until she finished a complete song. More often, she sculpted a tune with Gomez. Each offered input on lyrics and the shape and direction of the guitar accompaniment.

A finished track was the result of democratic cooperation.[27] Recording and live performance were the exceptions. Gomez preferred to play the guitar, and Sandoval agreed to sing. Together, they wrote original songs, some of which Mazzy Star would record ("Give You My Lovin") or plug into their setlist ("Where Did You Go?"). This process, which worked so well with Gomez, became the basis for the Sandoval and Roback partnership.

Early years spent woodshedding with Gomez proved fruitful. Eventually, the audience of one was not enough. In the pre-internet age, the two introverts could not stay in their bedrooms. Gomez and Sandoval began to sneak out of their homes to watch bands perform, daring to leave East LA to find their scene. Teenagers on the prowl for like-minded minds did not find it in the trendy West Hollywood. It was the start of the hair metal era. Thanks to the rise of So-Cal's Van Halen, bands like Poison and Mötley Crüe featured nightly at the Roxy and Whiskey a Go Go on the famed Sunset Strip. Sandoval and Gomez instead flocked toward small clubs where a group of musicians and bands resisted the crazes of MTV in favor of psychedelia, slow stretched-out jams, and melancholic malaise. It did not take long for Sandoval to single out musicians in her preferred scene. Most important was Kendra Smith, the bassist of The Dream Syndicate whose voice Sandoval once listed as a favorite beside Nina Simone and Billie Holliday.[28] Six years older and a known songwriter in LA's indie music scene, Kendra Smith was the ideal role model for a quiet female musician. Sandoval sat through Smith's soundchecks. She dragged her mother (and her mother's tamales) to Smith's concerts when she was too young for admission alone into a venue.[29] Friendship blossomed, and quickly, Sandoval and Gomez were in Smith's orbit, following her from show to show. It was especially inspiring to Sandoval that when Smith wanted to leave her band The Dream Syndicate and start another— she did. To start her next group, Smith worked on finding those who shared her vision. She wanted bandmates who were fascinated by the unfashionable Syd Barrett.[30] More importantly, she wanted those who did not resent working with women. Smith remembered someone who she once recorded for, someone who popped up in the same venues, and someone whose guitar-playing Hope Sandoval admired from afar. David Roback. By 1984, Smith and Roback along with drummer Keith Mitchell and organist Suki Ewers were performing as Opal. And as Smith and Roback worked to get their new band going, Sandoval and Gomez were inspired to do the same.

They called themselves Going Home. Their name referenced the Rolling Stones' track they played over and over in their bedrooms. In some sense, it was also a metaphorical comfort. If their plans did not work out, they could always withdraw to the safety of the indoors. There, however, was no need to immediately retreat. Around this period, events are muddled, timelines are mixed up, and accounts of Roback's involvement differ. Putting the consistent facts together, the story is as follows. Roback and Sandoval were aware of each other for years, passing through the same venues, hanging with mutual friend Kendra Smith, and having an interest in similar acts. But they rarely spoke to each other. Sandoval blames their few conversations and delayed friendship on their shyness.[31] The formation of Going Home provided the excuse to bring them together.

One of Going Home's earliest supporters was Kendra Smith. At some point in the band's early days, Smith received a tape of their demos. She passed it along to her new bandmate Roback who described the songs as "surrealistic folk music" that were "very spooky . . . "[32] Charmed by the music, and captivated by the vocals, Roback agreed to produce a demo. They recorded at the Radio Tokyo Studio.[33] Jane's Addiction, The Descendants, The Bangles, and Black Flag passed through the place. Even beyond the litany of who's who, it was an appropriate location for Sandoval and Gomez. The studio was in a nondescript house in Venice Beach. Recording there was not unlike being in their bedroom. Though talks have circulated over the years, an official release of this material has never seen the light of day. Bootleg copies now circulate online. Give it a listen and Sandoval seems fully formed. It's unbelievable how controlling that soft voice is, and how her odd, dreamy lyrics already contain a poetic power.

The next part of this story is absurd. Too astounding for a fictional script. On January 17, 1985, Going Home arrives at Hollywood's Anti-Club for just their third gig.[34] They open for Sonic Youth. They open for the Minutemen. They become reliable fixtures on the alternative music circuit. How did two shy precious teenagers who are outsiders in their neighborhoods, and who as Chicanas are outsiders in the music scene, find themselves as insiders in a network of prominent alternative bands in LA? An introverted woman who rarely replies to interviewers in whole sentences somehow seems to have not only hustled but hustled correctly? It is an intriguing and inexplicable side of Sandoval. The studio and the small venue must have freed her, and she must have found in both the opportunity to join a community that welcomed the reserved.

And so, Going Home has a studio tape. They have fans in the music scene and word of mouth. They are getting regularly booked to play in interesting venues with significant cult acts. There is, suddenly, a major problem. Going Home ends. There is no major drama. There is no bitterness or scorn on the record. Sylvia Gomez, despite her love of writing and performing music, wonders if there is not another purpose in her life.[35] She remembers the students in public school. What if her and Sandoval had an adult who cared, who better related to them, and who understood their community? Gomez went back to school, finished her degree, and devoted her life to teaching. Over the years, Sandoval's rare slips about her friend suggest Gomez had her blessing, and that the two have remained close. But one cannot properly speculate what went through Sandoval's mind in 1987. Surely, some part of her worried, or felt abandoned, or that the journey was momentarily lost? After all, she lost her friend and primary collaborator. All the momentum from the previous year stopped.

If there is a clue to the heartbreak of losing Gomez as a bandmate, it pops up in Mazzy Star's later "Blue Light." On *So Tonight That I Might See*'s middle track, Sandoval explores separation from a best friend. Just as Gatsby notices a green light on the dock near his far away love, Sandoval describes a blue light possessing her friend's eyes and room. It implies a deep sadness until Sandoval admits she wants "to see it shine," a clue that whatever sadness exist is temporary, a bittersweet truth that contains some good.[36] Meanwhile, Sandoval is in her own bedroom, watching a ship sail away and the waves crash on for miles. As the ship continues to shrink, a metaphor for the friend vanishing from her life, she admits to finding a world beyond the bedroom where there are "flames over everyone's heart."[37] She asks if her friend can see them shine. It's proof that what sparkles is not always positive. The song is a profession of support to Gomez and a profession of self-faith for Sandoval. Sadness can contain assurance. Light can contain darkness. Two truths can exist at once. It is how Sandoval regards the industry. The music business contains the opposite of what she loves in her friend: greedy misers and ungrateful souls. And yet, she wants to make her art. She pursues the dream capable of burning her. Because, as she declares, she wants to reach people's hearts and "hear them beating for me."[38]

Whatever Sandoval felt in the aftermath of Going Home's demise, she was not alone in the music scene for long. The Jesus and Mary Chain, who are hot off 1985's *Psychocandy* and are readying a tour to promote their upcoming album *Darklands*, want Opal to open for them across the United States and Europe. The tour kicks off in the Fall of 1987. But suddenly, after playing in Providence, Kendra Smith walked out and quit. In what may be a mere attempt to ramp up drama and intrigue, several publications suggested Smith's response was an emotional act, a furious reaction to some broken agreement.[39] Stoking these flames of intrigue is Roback's decision to phone Hope Sandoval and ask her to help them finish the tour. I suspect the rumors of heartbreak, of romantic entanglements, of a secret romance between David Roback and Hope Sandoval begins in these moments. Kendra Smith says otherwise. That her decision to quit was made because she hated touring. Besides Roback's call was not unusual given that Sandoval had a history of helping Opal in LA.[40] I will not speculate further on the gossip except to say it is impressive if there is drama that the involved parties remain silent. All I have are the facts.

Sandoval received Roback's message. She flew out to the East Coast and on November 20, 1987, at Detroit's St Andrews Hall, she played her first gig singing for Opal. It becomes her job. For two whole years, she does not perform her original music. She sings songs written for or by another woman.

III

By the end of 1987, the US music scene was primed for Latinos to stir their own path. While popular artists like Madonna peppered their music with the sounds of Latin America, and the Mexican American guitarist Dave Navarro emerged onto the LA music scene with Jane's Addiction, the largest surge of public interest in American Latine culture, emanates from the man who started it all: Ritchie Valens. In the summer of the same year, Columbia Pictures released *La Bamba*, a bio pic about the tragically killed Chicano rocker. The film coincided with a wave of increased nostalgia for the 1950s and followed hits *Back to the Future* and *Peggy Sue Got Married*. In addition, Chicano director Luis Valdez marketed the film to Latine-areas. Advertisers partnered with Latine journalists and schools across East LA to get the word out. In a remarkable first for Hollywood, Columbia Pictures offered the film in both English and Spanish.[41] For all the importance of these marketing stunts, a significant factor to the film's success was the music. Chicano and Latine musicians were at the forefront of an irresistible soundtrack. First, Mexican icon Santana teamed with Miles Goodman to compose an original score. Throughout the film, Santana's recognizable guitar-playing supplies a haunting omen to Valens's nightmares of flying and eventual demise to it. And second, the film updated Valens for a new generation. Los Lobos, an East LA Chicano band that had been active since 1973, was recruited to bring a harder, rougher edge to Valens's songs to recapture the electric shock of Valens's initial arrival. The result? Their cover of "La Bamba" reached the top of the charts, surpassing the original in sales. The film's soundtrack became a massive hit, selling two million copies within the United States.[42]

The success of *La Bamba* and its soundtrack suggested Chicano stories could find fans in and outside their ethnic communities. And, for a moment, Hollywood seemed interested. Over the next few years, more Chicano-centered films trickled into theaters (*Stand and Deliver*, *Born in East LA*, *American Me*). Let's remember, though, the Valens story is not just tragic, it's cursed. The burst of opportunity provided by the film was a short one. The soundtrack's success propelled Los Lobos to a sudden fame after almost fifteen years of critical praise but middling sales. They opened for Bob Dylan, U2, and the Grateful Dead. Audiences clamored for "La Bamba." An identity crisis followed for the band about how to escape from the shadow of being a mere tribute act, of reclaiming their artistic presence, and of creating a sound that mirrored the present.[43] To get their wish, they had to do what Valens was never afforded. They had to double down on their heritage. To exorcise the demon of the film, the band recorded a set of traditional Mexican songs beside a few originals of their own in 1988's *La Pistola y Corazon*. It never sold like the film soundtrack. It did however help them to carve out their own space. They proved a rule for a Latin musician: to get ahead requires moving backward.

Los Lobos were not the only Chicano artists haunted by the ghosts of a former singer. The affliction pained Hope Sandoval. Touring with Opal provided her a sliver of her dream. She was performing with musicians she liked and singing songs written by a woman she admired. Yet the thrill soon dissipated. So long as she participated in the group known as Opal, she would be stuck sharing another's soul. Reflecting on the tour to *POP* magazine, Sandoval shared her displeasure.[44] She wanted to forge her own identity in the music scene.

For all the problems they likely faced growing up as Chicanos, Los Lobos' founding members David Hildalgo and Louie Pérez were teenagers at the height of Chicano activism in the sixties. It is telling that when the band suffered an identity crisis, they retreated to what so many activists of that moment called on Chicanos to do—they retreated to the culture. On *La Pistol y El Corazon* they created an album driven by nostalgia. This Spanish music was the sound many in their Latine fan base remembered their elder family members listening to during their childhoods. They continue the legacy of the song "La Bamba," the fusion of Spanish language and guitar that was also practiced by Thee Midnighters and Santana.

Sandoval, let's remember, saw the slow decline of so much activism get replaced by crime. She needed to find her own expression. To do so required her to exert her own control over the shadow of history. Like Question Mark and the Mysterians, she chose to downplay her ethnicity in the pursuit of freedom and expression. It's not an isolated decision. If she's going to find an identity, if she's going to fight for her music, she's going to do it on her own terms. She borrows from the pasts, and she rejects it when she wants.

On the overlooked track "Unreflected," Sandoval details how if we become too consumed with the past, we fail to see warning signs in our present. The song is comprised of two distinct stanzas. In the first, Sandoval describes how a figure that refuses to reflect is gone from the present. This person is initially described with such vehemence that when the singer thinks about them in memory, she has no desire to speak with them. "We don't have much to say," Sandoval states.[45] She begins to repeat the remark then stops curiously short: "We don't have much . . ." Listeners eager to discover biography from lyrics might question if this song is about Kendra Smith, and if Sandoval expresses both remorse and happiness for her success by supplanting Smith. The second stanza, after all, becomes almost self-reflective: "follow anybody, is that what you do?"[46] Maybe the biographical reading is fair and true. But as the song continues, the gestures also become universal: "Now we know what we'll be in the past."[47]

Sandoval's sentiment presents the past as a thing solely to remember. It is a part of a story that defines the present. However, it doesn't end there. She ends on a beautiful refrain which reminds us that there is more to endure. She ends with the claim there is "another life that's left." If we apply it to her world in East LA, to the ongoing identity crisis which faced, and still faces Chicanos and Latinos and everyone, it's a bitter lesson to stop over-romanticizing the past. The sacrifices have been made. Promises were won and lost. What is left is a life still ahead, a life still to live. In a beautifully twisted sentiment, the song argues reflection is great, yet so is knowing when to "unreflect."

Sandoval demonstrated just that. After two years of touring with Smith's former band, Opal grew tired of living out a past. In 1989, they changed their name to Mazzy Star.

Wasted

I

When David Roback received a tape of original music by the unknown, newcomer band Going Home, he thought he was done with Los Angeles; he especially thought he was done with the artists of his hometown. He escaped the City of Angels and returned to Berkeley, a city that had become a home over the years since briefly studying art at UC Berkeley in the late seventies.[1] Los Angeles had become too consumed with scenes, musicians wanting to belong to a movement, and worse, the same musicians wanting ceaseless attention and critical validation. Then there was the ongoing violence. Everyday shootings and frequent break-ins consumed the late-night news. An ongoing crime wave contributed to LA's reputation as one of the most dangerous US cities of the eighties. LA was his original home, where he was from, and yet all its corners seemed to conspire to push him away.

Unlike Sandoval, who was raised to view the upheaval of the 1960s Chicano Movement as a hindsight force, something which happened when she was far too young to know the complexities of, Roback grew up in LA on the precipice of great transformation. Sandoval came of age around violence and, as a result, became suspicious of cheerful positivity, finding comfort and ease in the urban grunge. Roback believed ugliness contained beauty. That with the right attention, the beauty could grow into something meaningful. As Susanna Hoffs states, Roback was drawn to "looking for the single rose growing through a crack in the pavement."[2] But his hometown threatened his personal philosophy. A child throughout the sixties, he witnessed community and coalitions of the disenfranchised overcome the seediness of their circumstances. They organized for a better future and encouraged a movement toward equability. Then it came crashing down. The older he got, the less change he saw transpire in LA and California. Roback was eleven in 1969. It was the year a small army of the Los Angeles Police Department (LAPD) and forty Special Weapons and Tactics (SWAT) team members attacked the Black Panther headquarters in the majority Black neighborhood of Watts. It was the year the Manson Family committed seven murders. For a music-obsessed kid, it was the year John Lennon announced his separation from The Beatles. The reserved child entered his teenage years and watched as his LA heroes vanished. Jim Morrison died in 1971. Many of Love's original members left the band due to internal squabbles, drugs, and crime. Arthur Lee went solo, struggling to sustain a career, and the albums stopped coming.

Upon graduating from Palisades Charter High School in 1975, Roback left a city decaying into depravity, seeking quiet and a space to create. He expected the divorce to be a permanent one. First, he went to Carleton College, a small private liberal arts university in Northfield, Minnesota. The town could not have been more different from LA. It was an hour away from Minneapolis. It was freezing cold. It was tiny. The population did not crack 20,000. Leaving behind familiar faces and the constant sunshine granted him time to study art, and he flirted with becoming a painter. Roommates recall him drawing underneath a poster of Jimi Hendrix and listening to The Doors.[3] It was, however, too solitary of an environment, too cloistered from the larger world. The shy Roback, the kid who loved to study the minds of others, needed the freedom and space to create, but he needed to live around people to inspire him. He dropped out of Carleton College and ran off to New York.

New York, by many measures of living, was worse than LA. In 1975, the city was on the verge of bankruptcy. The ensuing fallout from near-fiscal catastrophe worsened ongoing problems of trash, transportation, and infrastructure. Many fled decaying buildings while crime and poverty skyrocketed. The future mayor Ed Koch blamed many of the problems on racial tensions.[4] Out of the marginalized living in rotting spaces and cheap rents emerged a rallying sound that channeled the voices of the economically depressed and the socially frustrated. Punk music in New York refused to soften what trouble was going on in the world. At the same time, it offered (white) outcasts a temporary reprieve from both mundane urbanity and its extremes, in turn forming a variety of social communities. As critic Patrick Deer puts it, the "punk's city was both a scene of violence and potential safety."[5] Hypnotized by the possibility of such contradictions, Roback came back to music as his preferred genre of expression. He gave up on pursuing painting to listen to the bands at the famed downtown venue CBGB. Patti Smith and Television convinced him to pick up the guitar again. He would add to the sound of emerging punk. He too had his disappointments and disillusionments to share, his feelings of alienation. There was just one problem. Roback put it, "when I picked up the guitar and started playing it, the music didn't come out sounding punk. It was something else."[6]

Once again, he felt lost. Roback found in punk a style which captured his unspoken voice, his longing for expression, and yet he was not an appropriate fit. He could not adapt his talent to the scene—or anyone. The portrait of himself as an artist was incomplete. He packed up his guitar and returned to university, transferring to UC Berkeley where his childhood friend Susanna Hoffs attended school. Hoffs was more than a familiar face. Similar to Roback, she studied art yet felt increasingly drawn toward pursuing music since a live performance by Patti Smith electrified certain neurons in her brain.[7] They became a couple and moved into a Victorian house the owners converted into an apartment.[8] The space was a laboratory for two young artists to practice and experiment with strange sounds and new techniques while providing one another crucial feedback. Originally, they called their duo the Psychiatrists, inspired by Roback's lifelong fascination with psychology and Hoffs's father who practiced psychoanalysis. It was a bit too on the nose. So, they changed their name to "the Unconscious."[9]

Stories abound about how Hoffs and Roback treated the Unconscious as an extended art project, developing heady audio and visual material to accompany the music.[10] Though Hoffs stated they never played live, other reports claim they performed in small and private sessions, timing their performances to last exactly fifty minutes—the length of a standard psychiatry appointment.[11] They recorded covers of favorite bands like the Velvet Underground and Nico, twisting and turning the sound with stressed, reverbed-out guitars to create a beautiful but melancholy sound that Hoffs argues was indicative of Roback's future in Mazzy Star.[12]

One of the dangerous truths about LA is that in a city full of hustlers and dreams, even the strongest bonds and relationships become vulnerable. Starting and sustaining a band is tough. Sustaining it with a significant other? In Los Angeles? Breakups are preordained. When Hoffs graduated from Berkeley in 1980, she and Roback were drifting apart as a couple and as a band. There was to Hoffs the feeling that the Unconscious was a phase, a season of youth which was ending. Back in LA, she found the thrill she desired in Berkeley. Musicians interested in combining the melodic hooks and chords of 1960s rock music with power pop emerged. Then there were the Go-Go's, an all-female rock band tearing through the city, attracting fans of punk and new wave. Hoffs was convinced. She needed to change direction. She needed a new band. Homemade flyers appeared in record stores and the famous venue Whiskey a Go Go. Hoffs took out an advertisement in the free newspaper *The Recycler* which called out for "GIRLS."[13] Two sisters, Viki and Debbie

Peterson, responded. In December of 1980, the sisters and Hoffs got together. They started as the Colours. Then the Bangs. Finally, The Bangles.

For those who know David Roback primarily through his interviews and performances with Mazzy Star, the guitarist appears like a soft-spoken sage. Responses to questions, while vague, indicate a deep intelligence derived from patience and reflection. And so, it can be hard to square this image with the artistic figure of the early eighties who, at any cost, exhibits a determination to become an artist free to experiment and create. But the stories of the era suggest there was, if not an anger, a sadness about Hoff's departure and worse, a resentful envy about her talent. Matt Piucci, Roback's friend from Carleton College, recalls going to a party in the Hollywood Hills to attend an early Bangles' gig (they were still known as the Colours). During their set, Piucci noticed that "David was crying" because he "couldn't take that his friend was going to be more successful than him right off the bat."[14] Roback was not content to go down without an effort. He joined Piucci's group Rain Parade and contributed what became their first single, "What's She Done to Your Mind," a song he wrote after the experience of watching Hoff's new band perform.[15] Roback's track describes a person who cannot convince himself to ignore the scars of a recent breakup. Authentic emotions rise to the surface. Tears form. The mind is a mess. Roback's downhearted lyrics are accompanied by an upbeat chiming guitar. It's a fusion perfected by his heroes The Beach Boys and Arthur Lee. And as the track moves into the chorus, Roback expresses his despondent anger in an unsubtle dig: "She can let you down."[16] Backing vocals repeat the refrain.

II

Like an author of genre fiction who resists bookseller efforts to wring them into a more marketable ghetto, who hates their classification as a *genre* author, the musicians associated with the Paisley Underground hated the term. It starts with the first word. The Paisley pattern is a design with origins in Persia and Southeast Asia. It was later appropriated in the West and popularized in the 1960s hippie subculture when bands like The Beatles embraced it after visiting India. To be lumped into a thing called the Paisley Underground suggested a retread of sixties enthusiasm for drug use, uninformed appropriation, and psychedelia. It narrowed dissimilar ambitions and influences to imply an inaccurate sense of collective identity. Critics on both sides of the Atlantic ran with the term to exploit the serious and social nature of the scene. Identification with the scene meant the musicians themselves became aware that a certain style and sound were expected, frustrating efforts to experiment and expand their range.

The term itself was an accident, an off-the-cuff quip put on page and set into motion in the minds of rabid music fans. Toward the end of 1982, a journalist from the *LA Weekly*—a free alternative newspaper which covers arts in the city—noticed friendship, romance, and camaraderie among several new bands who were performing across tiny venues in Hollywood.[17] These groups were The Three O'Clock, Rain Parade, The Dream Syndicate, and The Bangles. The journalist found Michael Quercio, The Three O'Clock's lead singer, and asked him what these musicians called themselves. Earlier on stage, he had come up with a phrase on the spot. Improvising a bit of spoken dialogue during a drawn-out instrumental climax of a song, Quercio recalled a friend's red Paisley dress purchased at a thrift store. It was part of their aesthetic. To purchase cheap leftovers from the sixties. The Paisley pattern of the dress slipped into his mind. The word underground came out of nowhere. On the stage, it sounded good, and it flowed, and it jokingly contained romantic gravitas. Don't we all think about those groups of artists—the Lost Generation in Paris, Beatniks in San Francisco, folk revivalists in Greenwich Village—hanging out, inspiring change, and redefining their cities? So, when the journalist asked Quercio for a name, it came back and never left: "the Paisley Underground."[18]

The Paisley Underground, despite being a disliked term by its participants, is useful in reflecting on this exact burst of creativity in early eighties Los Angeles. The name may have been an accident. The conditions and culture which brought these musicians together and pushed them to create were not. These were artists who came from middle-class backgrounds. Financial privilege occluded them from radical economic and cultural reactions. Sid Griffin, singer of The Long Ryders, theorized that the Paisley Underground was excluded from punk because their upbringings omitted them from a justifiable rebellion.[19] Freedom from financial precarity means the *LA Weekly* journalist who sought a name for these groups was right to believe in common throughlines. First, education played a major role in their development by freeing them from the pressures of an immediate job and by offering further education in exposure to canonical and experimental cultures. In fact, many of them initially met and formed their bands at universities outside of LA. We already discussed how Susanna Hoffs and David Roback reunited through UC Berkeley. Overlooked is the fact that Steven Roback, David's younger brother and Rain Parade bandmate, also attended the same school. Michael Quercio and his bandmate Louis Gutierrez flirted with junior college in between recordings. The Dream Syndicate's Kendra Smith and Steve Wynn met at UC Davis while working and running their own programs on the college radio station. Russ Tolman, whose band True West was often associated with the scene, also attended UC Davis and worked as a disc jockey. Sid Griffin came to LA to complete grad school at UCLA or USC when the DIY ethos of punk music convinced him to start a band. Whether they earned degrees or dropped out, education for the Paisley Underground meant finding common allies who were equipped to stir the pop music of the sixties in new, exciting, and experimental directions.

Second, the Paisley Underground is defined by Angelenos. David and Steven Roback, Susanna Hoffs, Michael Quercio, Louis Gutierrez, and Steve Wynn grew up in various neighborhoods of the city. Except for Quercio, they all left for multiple years to pursue higher education. As one of the older members, and as a dropout who fled to New York, Roback was one of the few to directly experience the enthusiasm of punk. The others, who stayed in school and were too young, only heard about the scene taking over their hometown. Stuck in their universities, they were separated from what they perceived was new and exciting. It fueled a desire for community and action of their own. The distance, in a sense, was a musical blessing. Proximity to the creators of punk might have altered their trajectory. The future members of the Paisley Underground might have fallen into a scene instead of creating a new one. Instead, most of their college years were a withdrawn period of autodidacticism. Radio DJs, coffeehouse musicians, and library rats, they filled the music hole in their hearts with avid record listening. As Quercio later put it, "we were all record collectors who played music."[20]

And finally, when many of these individuals came back home to LA to pursue music, their reason for moving was gone. They were outsiders in their own city. To those like Steve Wynn, punk and new wave were fading.[21] Other movements in the hardcore and art rock scene were unwelcoming. Why? Take a step back and consider the defining aspects of the Paisley Underground's output: long chords, 1960s garage and jangle rock, unstructured and elongated guitar-driven jams, vocal harmonies, and surreal soundscapes. Now, also recall what was popular the moment before their arrival. Van Halen emerged from the nearby town of Pasadena. Glam metal acts like Mötley Crüe dominated Hollywood's famous venues. Unpolished acts Black Flag and X intrigued many members of the Paisley Underground. At the same time, these groups were far too aggressive beside the Paisley Underground's softer sound and laid-back approach to performing.[22] Since MTV debuted in the late summer of 1981, The Cars, Duran Duran, and the Human League received significant screen coverage thanks to their bold sound and vibrant visuals. Go back to the restrained presence of Rain Parade on stage or the muted styles of The Dream Syndicate. It isn't hard to surmise that, as Steve Wynn states, to executives and general audiences of the moment, they "couldn't have been less fashionable."[23]

In its earliest stages, the Paisley Underground bands came together out of communal necessity. They were uncool music nerds who needed other acts to share the stage in small clubs, to help pay for rehearsal spaces, and to fill in on lineups when needed. All of which blossomed organically into them supporting each other and hanging out. In turn, they needed each other to help circulate word across town that something new was happening. Disagree or dislike the term, the Paisley Underground became a code for a secret society, a gathering for those who hated the processed music burgeoning on an upwardly popular MTV, a clubhouse for the outcasts too withdrawn for hardcore punk's violence, and a movement for those ready to explore the sun-damaged mind of LA.

III

To name an artistic movement is to announce the end of it. Media reactions to the news of a so-called Paisley Underground movement far outweighed general audience interest. The premier alternative LA rock radio station KROQ tried to hype up the scene. Radio DJ Rodney Bingenheimer, who made his name as an early adoptee of Blondie, the Sex Pistols, the Ramones, and so many others, teased The Bangles' first album *All Over the Place* (1984) with significant coverage.[24] The Dream Syndicate too were featured on Bingenheimer's program. Fanzines transformed into professional columns and spreads. Magazines based in other cities discussed the movement and likenesses in their local acts. New York media tried to lump Sonic Youth in the Paisley Underground. So too did journalists in Athens compare REM to Rain Parade. Others sought to link Minneapolis-St. Paul groups The Replacements and Hüsker Dü.[25] Critical discussion took off in the UK.[26] Listeners who flocked to new acts the Jesus and Mary Chain and My Bloody Valentine had found in the Paisley Underground the American counterparts who also mixed pop melodies with harmonic distortion and disinterested postures.

Critical attention did not lead to booms in sales or sustained success. It led to contracts. Major labels wanted to profit off this new, alternative market. Throughout 1983 and 1984, the courting began.[27] Island Records signed The Long Ryders and Rain Parade. The Dream Syndicate went to A&M, who were riding high on sales of Def Leppard. The Bangles, who were already an outlier because Columbia released their debut, signed on to be represented by Miles Copeland, who had clout in the industry due to also managing The Police. The Three O'Clock went with International Record Syndicate (I.R.S.), a relatively young but major subdivision of A&M that represented The Go-Go's.

Paisley Underground mania created trouble. Long before 1990s grunge ushered in the era of staying small, doing it yourself, and refusing to sell out, these LA bands did what they believed was expected. Major labels offered financial incentives, more opportunities, and the promise of bigger audiences. In short, the bands craved success. Another Angeleno named Dan Stuart, whose band Green on Red was forcibly lumped in with the scene, claims the surrender of artistic freedom for traditional success led to ugly disputes and intensifying rivalries. He explains it all on the fact "most of us were raised pretty bourgeois."[28] Pursuit of success and fame sent a wrecking ball through a once close-knit group of friends and allies. Performing on the same bill stopped. Rehearsals together died out. Unacknowledged in the demise of the Paisley Underground is also the importance of the 1984 Summer Olympics. Held in LA in late July and August, the ocean of tourists and athletes that descended on the city made it difficult to gather across the city. Increased surveillance and police presence in the months leading up to the games further limited the ability of young people to congregate.[29] Spikes in rent threatened small, independent venues. Getting out of the city was an economic and logistical must.

Efforts to popularize the scene led to extensive touring. Some, like Sid Griffin and the Long Ryders, found the long tours exhausting. Kendra Smith quickly dropped out of The Dream Syndicate to gain some peace from the road. Then there was an issue with marketing. The labels did not know how to advertise The Long Ryders or Girl in Red or The Dream Syndicate to listeners not in LA or New York.[30] Other groups became a bit glossier and more palpable to mainstream audiences in the Midwest. Miles Copeland worked his charm to secure a meeting with Prince and The Bangles.[31] It's an effort that created the latter's top hit "Manic Monday" on their second album *Different Light* (1986). The sleeker production is fascinating in its own way. It's hard to hear the same Paisley Underground group on chart-topper

"Walk Like an Egyptian," though "Walking Down Your Street" or "In a Different Light" retain the edge of earlier times. Others who did not do well were recycled by the industry. Michael Quercio and The Three O'Clock joined Prince and his new label Paisley Park Records in 1986. Though Prince gave them "Neon Telephone" to record for their third album, it gave them nothing more than a brief hope.[32] They became a commercial failure. And just like that, the Paisley Underground was done.

If you are wondering why I have not discussed David Roback much over these past paragraphs, it's because he, for better or worse, did not experience the mania. In 1984, at the height of major labels signing Paisley Underground acts, Roback's college friend and bandmate Matt Piucci fired him from Rain Parade. Reasons for the decision have changed over the years. Unflattering accusations that David Roback did not get along with his brother, that he wanted a larger say in the band's direction, and that he was too cryptic have all appeared in the press.[33] In a more recent admission to the *Los Angeles Times*, Piucci acknowledged that the firing permanently tainted their relationship. They were never friends again. Asked again about the split in 2020, Piucci explained, Roback was "going to be a famous artist no matter what," and that his determination to fulfill his dream created "collateral damage."[34]

Whatever the many reasons for the demise of the Paisley Underground, its true swan song is 1984's *Rainy Day*, a Roback-produced album that acts as a love letter to the music which inspired the scene's musicians, and a goodbye to his hometown. *Rainy Day* was recorded at Radio Tokyo in Venice Beach.[35] Roback gathered his friends: members of Rain Parade, The Three O'Clock, The Dream Syndicate, and The Bangles. Over a period of nebulous days, everyone contributed to a recording. By the end, there are covers of Bob Dylan, The Who, The Beach Boys, Nico, and more. One of the sweetest and most enjoyable covers is "I'll Keep it With Mine." Susanna Hoffs sings, and Roback plays guitar. They transform Nico's famously level vocals into the combined indulgence of two youths looking ahead. Hoffs almost appears to giggle at the end of some verses, and Roback's guitar is defiantly bouncy. Two friends are reuniting. Returning to a song that brought them together as kids. Looking ahead, considering how their lives may again diverge. As the song suggests, there is a place for each of them in their hearts that they will forever carry. A piece of them they will forever bring forward into their music. *Rainy Day* was released in 1984. It went out on shelves with no flair, collecting dust until the copies were gone. Roback's friends had abandoned him for major labels. He was, once again, left behind. He moved to Berkeley.

But he was not alone. Kendra Smith traveled north to speak with him. She possessed two important things: the desire to start a new band and a copy of Going Home's demo.

IV

Roback agreed to come out of retirement for the creation of Opal. In a sense, he shared with Kendra Smith a disappointment that the Paisley Underground scene devolved into a pursuit of fame and fortune through major labels. In addition, he shared with her a want to respond by succeeding on their terms. Opal freed Roback and Smith to pursue music without the constraints of being part of the Paisley Underground. They had a plan: "ow[n] their lives."[36] They had instruments and some empty rooms. What else did they need? They needed LA. Roback kept his home in Berkeley but ventured back in search of talented musicians. And as he had done at the decade's start, they placed an advert for bandmembers in the *LA Weekly*.

Reflections on this period reveal a more flexible Roback. Matt Piucci's account of Roback in Rain Parade describes a control freak who lashes out at any outside suggestion of change. The crew of Opal describe a figure who embraced a jazz mentality. Roback and Smith assembled a group where each member of the band might, at any moment, add their voice to the performance. In contrast to his early bandmates, Opal's keyboardist Suki Ewers and drummer Keith Mitchell remained lifelong friends and collaborators. Spurned by previous acts, Roback had, at long last, found a crew of musicians who functioned on his wavelength. Perhaps it was the fact that Opal marked a return for Roback to the folksy-blues sound of Love and The Doors. It was a return to the sounds which first attracted him to playing the guitar. Listen to their first and only album *Happy Nightmare Baby* (1987) and focus on the guitar. Roback's playing contains the thrill of a kid told to turn up the amp with abandon at a saloon. On "She's a Diamond," it would fit into a honky-tonk, while it titters on the edge of chaotic noise in "Supernova," and it pulls back to do both on "Siamese Trap."

Opal's *Happy Nightmare Baby* is a fascinating album. Hypnotic numbers are both sexy and dangerous. They evoke a psychedelic atmosphere fit for lucid dreaming. Kendra Smith also fills in apt and minimal vocals. Though, more often, the collective instrumentation is the intended force of effect. It is a perfect example to kick off a question: What could have been? But, if you will forgive my inserting an opinion, it's also easy to see the limits of such a band. Smith lacks Sandoval's poetic elocution. Opal's lyrics are plainspoken. Devoid of mystery. Sandoval transforms a single word into a puzzle of a deepening secret. Smith's vocals are regularly buried within the ocean of noise, while Sandoval's are waves, capable of signaling how calm precedes and shadows a storm. Opal's album nods to the coming rise of shoegaze. Yet somehow it feels trapped in the lo-fi noise of the Paisley Underground scene.

Opal's reputation suffers in hindsight of what is to come because of Smith's departure. Still, it is important to recognize that *Happy Nightmare Baby* primed audiences and media to fuel Mazzy Star's success. First, when Sandoval stepped into the abandoned role of lead singer, it was the opportunity to perform with a band that was a cohesive and professional unit. Roback was a seasoned veteran in the alternative scene. So was Keith Mitchell, who had drummed for Green on Red. Multi-instrumentalist Will Glenn, who helped in Opal, had experience working with Roback in Rain Parade. Sandoval was young in comparison. Though she founded and performed in Going Home, she had not toured extensively or worked in an ensemble that did not include her friend Sylvia Gomez. For all the pain of performing another's songs and not her own, Sandoval learned to avoid styles of singing that were uncomfortable for her. And so, performing in Opal was, in essence, practice that also granted her immediate access to a network of musicians like the Jesus and Mary Chain's brothers William and Jim Reid. These are people who knew how to navigate a studio, who knew names at independent labels, and who craved and cultivated small cults of their art.

And second, David Roback's reappearance on the musical scene caught the ears of English music magazines *Melody Maker* and *NME*. As previously mentioned, the Paisley Underground received significant coverage in Western Europe.[37] Rain Parade, in particular, was reviewed with critical fervor. *Emergency Third Rail Power Trip* (1983) earned cult status among alternative listeners who highlighted Roback as a creative force. Further, releasing the limited Roback-Smith single "Fell from the Sun" in 1984 through the London-based record company Rough Trade resulted in anticipation in the UK for his next project. Journalists in their home country also snapped to attention after the announcement that Opal would tour with the Jesus and Mary Chain whose debut *Psychocandy* (1985) and follow-up *Darklands* (1987) created scores of intrigue among alternative music fans and the music press.

Let us also not underestimate the drama of it all. Because so many critics and journalists expected to review Opal's tour and their album, Smith's sudden and unexplained departure created a tabloid-level frenzy. The music press and Opal's fan base believed themselves entitled to answers. Who was this new singer named Hope Sandoval? What had happened between Kendra and David? Between Kendra and Hope?

Which singer did fans prefer? Irresistible possibilities of an inner scandal led to article after article about the group's new identity. *Spin* magazine in the United States, *Melody Maker* and *NME* in the UK, and Germany's *Spex* rushed to explain where Hope Sandoval came from throughout 1988 and into 1989. Importantly, they rushed to photograph this mysterious new singer. So many of the images, black-and-white or grainy, make you hungry to know more. For all the likely pressure created by the media's assault on their personal lives, Sandoval and Roback refused to break. In interviews they teased out their relationship, frustrated editors with opaque clues about Opal's future, and mystified concertgoers who discovered a new, calmer sound when they expected the garage-rock psychedelia of Smith's Opal. Before all the goodwill was up, before the intrigue died, and before editors moved on to the next hot new alternative act, they announced a new identity and album. Mazzy Star was born.

She Hangs Brightly came out on May 21, 1990, by Rough Trade Records. Recorded mostly in San Francisco, with some tracks redone in a studio in Venice, California, the album is a phenomenal and astounding debut.[38] The track "Halah" is an immediate standout. The album's opener mixes Roback's psychedelic interest with Sandoval's folksy-blues past to create a beautiful acoustic track about bitter and hopeful regret over a lost lover. Listening to the song is the equivalent of overhearing a vulnerable confession between two sober friends. It would be voyeuristic if not for the fact it's so sensual. I'm not sure the album sustains this high. Their follow-up "Blue Flower," a cover of a forgettable 1972 song from the German/English art-pop group Slapp Happy, is clearly the effort of a band working to make a palpable radio hit.[39] It's catchy and charming. Sandoval's vocals are smooth and refined. While the rest of the album has the quality of catching a band in a coffeehouse, "Blue Flower" is the one track on the album that feels like it comes from a studio. Never again are Mazzy Star so close to embodying a pop-rock band. Unsurprisingly, "Blue Flower" was and is a favorite among listeners.

Listening to *She Hangs Brightly* is to rediscover a band still learning to blend its influences. Of the eleven songs, four belong to ghosts. In addition to "Blue Flower," the album also features a rendition of Memphis Minnie's blues classic "I'm Sailing." One conjectures that Roback selected Slapp Happy and Sandoval chose Memphis Minnie to cover. Similarly, each of the pair brought in one tune from their previous bands. They recorded a Sylvia Gomez track entitled "Give You My Lovin'" and a Roback-penned tune for Opal called "Ghost Highway." The result of this approach is that the Roback-Sandoval tracks can feel disjointed from these others and the album as a whole, especially its second half, loses focus. Latter songs like "Taste of Blood," "Free," and "Before I Sleep" are effusive exercises in creating a gloomy atmosphere. But that mood remains the same. Apart from the underrated "Be My Angel," Mazzy Star's originals tend to dissolve together. As a result, I do not think it is a coincidence that, minus "Halah," fans tend toward listening to the covers and more refined tracks carried over from Going Home and Opal.

I hope it does not appear that I am dismissing *She Hangs Brightly*. There is an effort in the sound to distinguish themselves while contributing to a canon of dreamy music.

For that reason, I too love the album. I have returned to it countless times. If I am being honest, on some days, I might rank it above *Among My Swan*. Blasphemy, I know! But the weaknesses I find might best be expressed by discussing the cover art. The cover, created and chosen by Roback and Sandoval, is a blue-tinted photo of a stairwell at the Hotel Tassel in Brussels. The stairwell looks abandoned. Beside it is a lift covered in shadow. Iron ornate railing abounds. The setting has the appeal of a haunted, gothic house fit for Vincent Price. It's a purposeful choice. The Hotel Tassel's interior is renowned for bringing in natural light. Mazzy Star transforms it into the scene of abandonment. They create their own stunning architecture. But they refuse to bring in the light. They prefer to remain insulated in their enclosed world. Call me naïve, someone who wants to notice some sun served with my melancholy. *She Hangs Brightly* is simply too concerned with flirting in the dark. If you find my reasoning flawed, you are not alone. Better individuals than I have cherished the album. Kurt Cobain scribbled in his notebooks that *She Hangs Brightly* was one of his fifty favorite albums.[40] In contrast to their first album, *So Tonight That I Might See* explores the duality of emotion by breaking out of the entrapments of their own gloomy architecture. It is the album from two observers who overcome alienation in each other. It is an album in which each partner reflects on what had become of their hometown.

But before I get to this argument, it is important that I share that *She Hangs Brightly* is not a commercial success for Rough Trade. It continues Roback's reputation for projects which critics adore and wide audiences ignore. There is a good chance that Mazzy Star might have also continued the tradition of Roback's bands as one-album-and-done groups. On May 21, 1991, almost a full year since *She Hangs Brightly* debuted, Rough Trade declared bankruptcy. For the rest of 1991 and 1992, Mazzy Star withdrew from the stage. There were no shows planned. They had no clear future. The members retreated from live performance. Sandoval traded the harshness of her old neighborhood for the anonymity of a pre-gentrified Silverlake in LA. Roback, as he had done whenever his path was uncertain, returned to Berkeley.[41]

Then LA came calling—again. It came calling in the form of big business. Capitol Records, a major label who had published The Beach Boys and handled the US distribution for the Beatles, bought up Mazzy Star's contract.[42]

The Capitol Records Tower famously stands in the northern section of Hollywood. A thirteen-story office building which coincidentally resembles a stack of records on a turntable. It is a famous landmark in a city not known for tall, eclectic architecture. Visible from most Hollywood streets and the freeway, it was the dominant sight in an area of town where few other buildings stretched toward the sky. The fact says it all: Capitol Records was the big name in a show business city. All those nights Roback and Sandoval played in tiny venues and rundown clubs? Capitol Records looked down like the eye of Sauron.

1991 had ushered in a new frontier. Nirvana's "Smells Like Teen Spirit" and the sudden success of *Nevermind* in the fall of the same year taught executives that underground music could reach mass audiences. Better yet, that it could move plenty of albums off shelves. Capitol Records, one of the biggest labels in the country, wanted in on the action. The ensuing madness to market and profit off underground acts startled Roback. Capitol's relentless push made the contractual grabs of the Paisley Underground seem innocent. The record company started by re-releasing *She Hangs Brightly* in 1992.[43] They also issued copies of a new song "She's My Baby" with "Halah" to radio stations and college newspapers. The DJs ignored the intended single in favor of the B-side. Three years since its initial release in 1990, "Halah" earned a spot on airwaves and rotated in the late hours of MTV.

But Capitol Records wanted more. They exhausted the existing material. What else was there? Mazzy Star were about to deliver on the question. It is essential that we consider the fact that in the years between their first and second album (1990–3), Roback and Sandoval enjoyed a level of freedom that is now uncommon in the music business. Renewed sales on *She Hangs Brightly* and a major label contract led to an increase in money. That bought them freedom from work, from giving interviews, and from touring where they could lay low and experiment with new ideas without burnout and frustration. There was also the fact that a frontier is a lawless, untamed, and uncertain landscape. In the early 1990s, record companies did not know how to manufacture the underground sound that was dominating the charts. Capitol took a hands-off approach in the recording process. As Roback later described, it was a short-lived period when major labels believed they should "let [bands] do what they need to do and leave them alone, and they'll make a good record."[44]

To record Mazzy Star's follow-up, Roback needed to go home. Though Capitol was content, for the moment, to give them their freedom, Roback remained suspicious of businessmen and executives. In order to preserve their sound and their artistic identity, Roback wanted to produce and mix the album himself. Recording in LA meant confronting a changing city and confronting old ghosts. The Paisley Underground had been over for a decade. Mazzy Star would not look backward. Then they would enact a different step. If not forward, then to somewhere new. But everything seemed to suggest doom. The year 1992 was and is the most violent year in Los Angeles County's history. It was the year of the South Central Riots, when more than 10,000 armed responders descended on the city to stop the rioting of thousands who were upset after a jury acquitted four officers in the beating of Rodney King.[45] And they were going to record an album? Roback's hero Arthur Lee did not shy away after witnessing the Watts Riot of 1965. If Roback and Sandoval were going to do so, they had to make a statement about their city. It was not a moment for detachment.

Out of this despair and change, two frequent outsiders came together to record *So Tonight That I Might See*. After its release, *NME*'s journalist Danny Frost pushed Roback and Sandoval on their hometown city, asking about its shallow and plastic reputation. Sandoval muses about what has all transpired to note, "I think it has become alienating."[46] The camaraderie of the Chicano uprisings and movements was all gone, and working people were scattered and suffering and searching for hope. Roback, meanwhile, offered a challenge: "LA is a cancer patient, it's riddled with cancer, but you don't put cancer patients down, you fight to make their lives a little better."[47] For their second album, Mazzy Star remain aware that LA—that the world—is a dark place. Yet in Roback and Sandoval, there is the comfort of two quiet souls and one dream coming together to make their lives, and ours, "a little better." However alienating the world, however alienated we feel as individuals, and however alienated we feel from making a difference, it's worth pushing on.

So Tonight That I Might See

I

David Roback and Hope Sandoval wanted out of their Capitol Records contract.[1] Pressure to follow their sophomore effort and to do it with haste was the opposite of how they approached their art. Executives at the record label were growing impatient. They wanted to remain hands-off and retain the band's underground charm. Yet they also wanted a higher return on their investment. So far, their slow approach to marketing Mazzy Star had paid off. A year after its initial release, the RIAA certified *So Tonight That I Might See* Gold for 500,000 copies sold in the United States. By its second anniversary in 1995, the RIAA certified it Platinum for selling over a million copies.[2] The sales—on one released music video—surely astounded Capitol's marketing team. Why not cash in? Why not hurry to build on the momentum? This moment, importantly, was the era when female-fronted alternative groups gathered new fans from the mainstream. To name a few: The Cranberries, The Sundays, Hole, Garbage, Sleater-Kinney, PJ Harvey, The Breeders, and The Cardigans. Many of these groups worked with their record companies to craft chartable hits. Many of the women fronted music videos. Hell, even underground god Kim Gordon of Sonic Youth partnered with major label Geffen Records to deliver albums *Goo* (1990) and *Dirty* (1992) during this period. So why were Mazzy Star so reticent to proceed? Why did they reject nearly all media promotion? Why were they so desperate to escape from the suits at Capitol Records?

To answer such questions requires examining the cultural forces of *So Tonight That I Might See*'s era to better understand how such a quiet and isolating band found a large audience. "Fade into You" is part of this recipe (as discussed in Chapter 1). However, a brilliant and unforgettable single is not the whole story. Marketers sold "Fade into You" to teenagers. They grabbed their attention and more. An audience varied in age, race, and gender flocked toward the album. Perhaps the biggest demonstration of this diverse support came from the future criminal mastermind Martha Stewart, who included the album as a must to accompany dinner parties.[3] (I do wonder what sort of dinner parties necessitate "Into Dust"). Other evidence of their widespread appeal is their soundtrack appearance in two distinct films: *Batman Forever* in 1995 and *Stealing Beauty* in 1996. In one, they appear in a cartoonish action blockbuster and, in the other, an art house film from Bernardo Bertolucci, a favorite film auteur among the baby boomers. Oh the 1990s, when a slow Mazzy Star number seemed a good fit for Val Kilmer's Batman! Mazzy Star can reflect the cartoonish world of Batman's Gotham and summon the anguish of a teenage girl coming of age in the Italian countryside.

And so, I write the following sentence without irony. Both appearances are a testament to Mazzy Star's power: their sound is out of place and out of time. To borrow a statement from journalist Annie Parnell, the irreplicable combination of influences in Roback and Sandoval "lends the work both a nostalgic quality and a timeless one."[4] In a sense, Mazzy Star have more in common with the strange, unsettling, and beautiful world of David Lynch's *Twin Peaks*. Theirs is also a universe where everything feels old and new at once. They exist to seemingly exemplify the late critic Mark Fisher's concept of hauntology, a theory about how art can dedicate itself to life's ephemeralness while also haunting us with the futures and pasts we wanted but never had.

Sure, female-led bands were on the rise in these years. But imagine Mazzy Star on a lineup with some of these acts. It's hard to say Mazzy Star fits in with the anguish and anger of Courtney Love. Nor does it match Dolores O'Riordan's confident yodeling while fronting The Cranberries. More pop-oriented entertainers Alanis Morissette and Fiona Apple, who released their debuts in 1995 and 1996, are too of-their-moment. To put it bluntly, their songs sound like the mid-1990s. Compared to the angsty grunge staples dominating the alternative charts during their rise, Mazzy Star are far too mellow, and far more feminine. Because the band recorded *So Tonight That I Might See* after a lengthy hiatus from touring, they settled for a largely acoustic recording, giving the album the feeling of an intimate bedroom concert. The anachronistic and personal nature compared to their contemporaries granted Mazzy Star the chance to extend their fan base in ways other groups could not. Take a song like "Unreflected." Roback strums in a manner fit for Patsy Cline while Sandoval passes for a more melodic Lou Reed. Anguish and contempt-soaked lyrics divulge Gen-X frustrations. In short, the song combines and crosses generational soundscapes.

Then there is the flow of the album. It is far more approachable than its reputation suggests. Following "Fade into You" is the irresistible tune "Bells Ring." Echoes of "Halah" in the soft strumming and Sandoval's near-whisper explain why the label did not push harder for it as a single. Though an acoustic performance on MTV Europe's Most Wanted in 1994 indicates there was some effort to sell the song. The camera constantly moves toward Sandoval in her light dress and black boots before slowly zooming out. It's close enough to keep an audience entranced. The distance ensures Sandoval does not wilt under scrutiny. It also makes us ashamed, as if we pried where we should not. Even without visual accompaniment, "Bells Ring" channels heartbreak from the heartbroken. Sandoval describes the chime of nighttime bells as akin to "sounds like a mistress on a rainy night."[5] Images of flowing water evoke dark romances worthy of a Brontë sister. I am tempted to propose it channels the same tragic idealization of John Everett Millais's *Ophelia*, a painting which depicts Shakespeare's Ophelia drowning in a river surrounded by lush greenery after Hamlet accuses her of wrongdoing. It's a haunting scene and overly interpreted with ironic cool girl energy in today's meme culture as romantic. Sandoval presciently taps into the ways the exaggerated emotion of youthful heartbreak calls for a teen tendency toward glamorizing gloom. Brilliantly, she sings with absolute sincerity. Sandoval aligns herself with the mistress when she asks an unforgiving soul to "leave my heart down by the water."[6] Wherever her tormenting lover goes, she tells him to observe the water, and "hold your hands out" to "know I'm with you."[7] The tormented mistress shall linger as a presence. As she closes the song, she announces she "just want[s] to be right by your side."[8] It's not played out for defeat; it is an announcement of emotional confidence. Roback's guitar swells. Electric notes held out for a slow cathartic effect filter into the airwaves.

The sound goes out, and we bask in a silent euphoria. Suddenly, a humming begins to vibrate. The next journey is far less sweet. If love can inspire supernatural devotion, it can also inspire violence. "Mary of Silence" is a six-minute slow jam. It's a slow and foggy number about a girl who is defined by nicknames about her sweet and quiet nature. Yet her actions denote a sinister contradiction. Mary snaps toward evil like Stephen King's Carrie. She devours hearts with "a smile."[9] She can take over bodies. The speaker describes Mary with trepidation, and the longer the song goes, the more the listener expects a dark climax. There isn't one. We emerge into a bright world. Their warm cover of Arthur Lee's "Five String Serenade" begins.

An accusation often lobbied at the band is that the music is too miserable. That it is music which revels in gloomy melancholia. When asked about the criticism on Musique Plus, a Montreal-based TV channel, Sandoval responded, "That's part of reality. Sometimes life is dark."[10] The confrontation and willingness to engage in the dark sides of life is present in "Mary of Silence." It's also there in later songs like "Wasted," which carries a hard-hitting and consistent guitar beat comparable to a drunken stagger through a dive bar. The lyrics suggest a realization about this defeat and the difficult effort to escape it. But the key word in Sandoval's response is that life is dark *sometimes*. In a separate interview, Roback offered a more complicated comment on their sound: "I think one of the great misconceptions people have about what is called melancholy music is that it's negative."[11]

Contrary to popular criticism, the album's engagement with the dark is matched by its pursuit of pleasure, both carnal and ethereal. "Blue Light" channels the want to embrace a friend during their rough period. It's a sweet sound which dissolves toward the atypical anguish of "She's My Baby." The bleakness of "Into Dust" is followed by the album's title track in which Sandoval slips into a witchy incantation to plead for some light to break through the gloom. Tracks flow from the soft to the loud and back, bearing witness to a range of darker emotions and a sudden need for happiness. It's a melancholy which knows there is an escape. It's a melancholy which recognizes it is sometimes good to listen to dark music. And it's a melancholy which seeks out the possibility of bliss.

Hope Sandoval's contribution to the band's aura, as both lyricist and reluctant frontwoman, helps to celebrate those artists unafraid to embrace sensitivity. Here is a working-class Chicana, born on the wrong side of town, baring all sides to the misery and ecstasy of what it means to simply be a human being. Whoever you are, it is alright to *feel*.

All of this leads me to complicate Mazzy Star's reputation as a miserable act for Sad Girls. The notion of Mazzy Star as a canonical band of Sad Girl music has followed them since the apex of their early fame. In 1996, *Alternative Press'* cover story declared Sandoval a "queen" of the Sad Girls.[12] Sad Girl music for the uninitiated refers to (mostly) female artists who sing of anguish, expressing their heartbreak and anger with vulnerable lyrics suggestive of pages freshly ripped from a diary. Though it originates from the 1990s boom of female alternative artists, it is not an exact genre.[13] Depending on the person, figures as far apart as Michelle Zauner of Japanese Breakfast and Nico might make the cut, while Mitski, Weyes Blood, and Lana Del Rey are frequently named. Then and now, the Sad Girl label is often bandied about as an ironic insult. In the decade when it emerged, the male-perpetuated term poked fun at the teenager who perfected their pout, who created collages out of their idols in their notebooks and lockers, and who clutched onto tragic poets Nick Drake or Jeff Buckley as dream boyfriends. More recently, it belittles the young woman who once flocked to Tumblr or Pinterest to reshare common images: Sylvia Plath quotations, rainswept London or Paris, and French New Wave starlet Anna Karina. The sort of young woman who idolizes the pink moodiness of Sofia Coppola's *The Virgin Suicides* and *Lost in Translation*. Lost in the process of simplifying this scene into a memeable stereotype is that the slight renders female-led interests in the arts as shallow. Worse, it homogenizes a scene full of diverse musicians into an image built around superficializing and prioritizing the white, thin, and middle-class woman. To insultingly declare music as meant for Sad Girls thus erases the race and class of artists like Hope Sandoval. It undermines how the most powerful of Sad Girl music contains a universalizing ability to empower those from dissimilar backgrounds.

Sad Girl music offers women comfort in knowing the world is, at best, indifferent to their concerns, and at worst, hostile to their needs. Sad Girl music accepts emotional outbursts and numbness. The ultimate reward of these expressions is a communal relief. Here are other women who share the same contradictory feelings about the world. Here are others who also believe in the importance of introspection. As such, the Sad Girl transcends the normal barriers between generations and class because these key themes are universal and unchanging.

In other words, the Sad Girl does not reinvent herself; she simply reoccurs. It is why artists from decades past, like Carly Simon, Joan Baez, Joni Mitchell, and Carole King, are lumped into this categorization. Specific proof of this claim lies in the early 2000s young adult soap classic *The O.C.*, which is about teenagers navigating romance and temptation in a rich and beautiful but artificial upper-class community. Ten years since the song's initial release in 1993, an episode of the program used Mazzy Star's "Into Dust" to soundtrack iconic Sad Girl Marissa Cooper's drug overdose during a Spring Break trip to Tijuana, Mexico.[14] The show portrays her accident as an exaggerated accumulation of normal teenage troubles: an unreliable boyfriend, distracted parents divorcing, and indifferent classmates. As the song plays, her friends find her. Terrified expressions pass over their youthful faces, and for all the isolation supposed by the Sad Girl identity, the combination of song and scene insinuates a reality that Mazzy Star also embraced. Keep close those few who truly understand and appreciate you.

Importantly, Sad Girl music does not limit itself to female listeners. It does not want to remain insular. It wants others to bear witness to female trouble. Let's recall that in the early 1990s, as Generation X entered their teenage years and young adulthood, there was a widespread recession in the United States and a growing disillusionment with the Wall Street hedonism which defined the previous decade's hair metal and visual culture of excess. Such factors are widely circulated as reasons for grunge's popularity.[15] Public cynicism about the mainstream and a carefully managed image gave Mazzy Star credibility in this cultural moment. Sad Girl vibes, several years before Fiona Apple's debut, importantly gave them access to women who shared grunge's angst but were alienated by the machismo of the genre's fans. And while grunge refuted expectations of the strong, silent male to divulge how frustration leads to rage and depression, Sad Girl music shares that such sad emotions are worth examining for their potential joy. This separation allowed the female-fronted groups to escape from grunge's descent into the mediocrity of the male malaise which characterized so much of the decade's post-grunge output.

A negative trait of Sad Girl music is when it becomes too much about aesthetics. There is a cruel irony that the Sad Girl commits a wrongdoing frequently associated with an overzealous and sexual male fan: hyperfocus on Hope Sandoval. Countless videos abound online of young women who seek to replicate the distant gaze, casual indifference, and aloof coolness of Sandoval. Trouble occurs from such a movement because it invites passive spectatorship. In doing so, it cheapens the anger at the world's indifference to female struggles by commodifying and strengthening the very lookism these artists have sought to undermine. But there is also something worth celebrating about these reproductions of Sandoval's aloof aesthetic that have helped to circulate Mazzy Star's music to diverse corners of the internet. Without Sandoval's role in Mazzy Star to crack the white homogenization of this loose and unofficial genre, future Sad Girls Karen O of the Yeah Yeah Yeahs, Michelle Zauner of Japanese Breakfast, and Mitski would have struggled to find their diverse audiences. In addition, Sandoval's Sad Girl pose teaches one that they do not need to disavow their feelings. She refused to perform for the lurid gaze of a male-dominated press. She embraced careful silence. Sandoval's silence was and is a power accessible to women across the globe. The Sad Girl belongs to everyone.

II

The *So Tonight That I Might See* era contains many hints at what the band might have become if they chose to pursue global fame. One senses there were ceaseless attempts to capitalize on Sandoval's appearance and transform her into a female Kurt Cobain, equally sensitive, introverted, and indifferent to fandom. One also senses that Capitol Records wanted her to become Fiona Apple, indifferent to the supposed tastemakers of what is cool, a popular figure in videos and magazines, and a headlining commercial star who moved tickets and albums.

It is most evident in the unreleased video for "She's My Baby," in which Sandoval and Roback are stuck inside a brown-gray home. Roback hovers in the background, clinging to his guitar, as if without it he would shrink and dissolve from the camera's attention. Undoubtedly, the emphasis is on Sandoval in a plain white dress. In between close-ups of her, the audience gets a twisted glimpse of objects and art typically associated with femininity. Floral wallpaper lines a bedroom wall. Vintage dolls are broken and cracked. Images of a blonde pin-up cartoon girl flicker by and never stop. Then there are the profound close-ups of Sandoval herself. In an early shot, we see her lounging, her legs bare beneath the dress. Remarkably, it's not sexually suggestive. It's playful. She reaches for an ankle bracelet and tugs. Other shots highlight the slow movement of her hands, the twisting of her hair, and her turning away. We want to see more of her, and she does not want to remain seen. She can momentarily fulfill the requirements of her record contract. However, she is not willing to play a doll, to give up control, and let others direct her movements. The final images of the video become foggy, and a film projector runs out of film. Once the entertainment ends, it ends.

Capitol Records surely would have liked to use this video to market the band. As defiant as Sandoval acts, it still capitulates to the corporate cynic who sells a band on the beauty of its Sad Girl frontwoman. Radio DJ and audience preference for the B-side single "Halah" paused its release.[16]

It did not truly matter. There were other ways for the record company to exploit her image for attention. Sometimes, the executives did not need to do a thing.

Mazzy Star came into existence during a tour with the Jesus and Mary Chain. Members of both bands never forgot each other. Friendships formed. And, in the case of Hope Sandoval and the Jesus and Mary Chain's lead guitarist William Reid, so too did romance. While the two often denied their romantic relationship with claims of friendship, rumors of their involvement fed many tabloids hungry for a story. Kurt Cobain and Courtney Love. Kim Gordon and Thurston Moore. Perhaps Reid and Sandoval were the next alternative-rock marriage waiting to happen. A romantic duo for all the shy and awkward kids.

Fans and writers eager for a scoop did not have to wait long. In the summer of 1994, several months after the official video release of "Fade into You," and just as the song was starting to catch public attention and enter the charts, the Jesus and Mary Chain released the mesmerizing "Sometimes Always." Meant to replicate the wistful and charming romantic playfulness of Nancy Sinatra and Lee Hazlewood collaborations, the song features Sandoval singing the lead part of a jilted girlfriend.[17] William Reid, who wrote the song, has his brother Jim act opposite her, pleading for her forgiveness and return. The song is a knockout, a lighthearted and catchy pop number neither artist is known for writing. According to the brothers, the collaboration was an event long in the making. Sandoval enjoyed speaking with the brothers, touring with them, and watching them fight and compromise with their engineers—and each other—to achieve their desired sound. For the collaboration to come when it did meant positive ongoing publicity for Mazzy Star as their star started to climb. Record executives would have described it to audiences as follows: it meant more Hope.

On September 9, 1994, the Jesus and Mary Chain release their music video for "Sometimes Always." It premieres just six days after "Fade into You" debuts on the Billboard Hot 100. The single is not a runaway smash, but it does crack the music charts in the United States and sells well in the UK.[18] It also becomes a remarkable cult favorite among alternative fans. For those waiting for Sandoval and William Reid to drive their fantasies of rock-and-roll romance, the video raises heartbeats. Both brothers sit next to Sandoval in a wooden dive bar as she disparages what the boyfriend in her life failed to do, and when Jim Reid replies, she slyly breaks the fourth wall to offer a smile. As the song progresses, the video features the three wandering a desert landscape. All of it feels like a straightforward sequel to the "Fade into You" video, as if Sandoval recorded both on the same day. Both the video and lyrics to "Sometimes Always" suggest William Reid wants people to see Sandoval with the same mesmerized longing he does.

If fans eager to ship the romance were not satiated by the music video, then a month later came a remarkable performance at MTV Studios. Never again in a live setting is Sandoval so well-lit. Sharing a stage with the Jesus and Mary Chain, she stands passive at the microphone, barely moving away to sing. Beside the Reid brothers, her bored posture looks natural. Despite, and because of, the indifferent attitude, the performance is brilliant. Watch it and one understands the creative power in those reportedly too antisocial and too self-motivated. These are artists who are creating for their pleasure and in return, giving us a taste of beautiful simplicity and earnestness. We want to witness it. We want to be in that audience. After the release of the collaboration, and after "Fade into You" first climbed into the Billboard charts, Mazzy Star and the Jesus and Mary Chain toured together in the Fall of 1994 across the United States. The combined tour culminated with a final pair of concerts in Los Angeles. At the end of November, "Fade into You" peaked at No. 44 on the Billboard 100.[19] "Sometimes Always" had fallen off the charts. In December, Mazzy Star performed on their own. Rumors have it, by then, William Reid and Hope Sandoval had broken up.[20]

Gossip about an alternative-rock romance, word of mouth about a brilliant second album, and a successful radio and MTV campaign all fueled attention toward Mazzy Star. They might have survived a bit longer in the public consciousness if they could have remained a band who toured historic venues of no more than five thousand people. In other words, if they could have remained your favorite artist's favorite artist, the suffering of the spotlight might have been tolerable. In this scenario, they tour with spiritually similar groups Cocteau Twins or the Jesus and Mary Chain, release albums on a timely yet respectful schedule, and interview once or twice for promotion. Capitol Records, for all their talk of leaving the band alone, made them increasingly uncomfortable.

Executives and media insiders flooded their shows. Capitol Records pretended to acquiesce to their demand for more intimate venues by booking Mazzy Star to play 300-person clubs.[21] When the band got there, it would be filled with industry heads who cared for the music only as background noise to their meetings and deals. These compromised showcases infuriated Roback and Sandoval. Whenever they complained, the label fought back with accusations of their difficult behavior. They leveled complaints to the press that Sandoval was a diva.[22] In 2001, Sandoval and Colm Ó Cíosóig, drummer of My Bloody Valentine and member of Sandoval's project The Warm Inventions, conversed about their frustration with the newspaper *East Bay Express*. Each of them shared how the experience of performing for businessmen was akin to "playing in courts for kings and queens like a minstrel or a bard."[23] For a group who demanded attention and quiet from an audience, continuing to play the part of bard was unthinkable.

Recording their follow-up *Among My Swan* also had its own challenges. Capitol Records learned the wrong lesson from Sandoval's successful single with the Jesus and Mary Chain. They encouraged other collaborations and pushed for Roback and Sandoval to hire an outside producer with a famous name. In a 2009 interview with the *Los Angeles Times*, Sandoval stated her perspective on this struggle: "I wanted to produce my music, and [Capitol Records] weren't having that. I'm sure they were happy to let me go. I just didn't want to do what they wanted me to do."[24] Roback and Sandoval held onto their creative vision. They refused to sit and write "Fade into You" part two. They refused to trim songs to radio-friendly lengths. Roback defended their slow and gloomy sensibility by claiming, "People have a lot of different interests in music, and I think that a lot of times that's forgotten, because maybe that's not where the money is happening."[25] The intention was clear. They defined the music they put out into the world. Still, their contract demanded it sooner rather than later. Against their wishes for time and against the odds, the Rip-Van Winkle band were pushed to waken and put their art into the world.

III

Among My Swan was released on October 29, 1996. It is a phenomenal album, a dark and moody masterpiece fit for a wintry night. For almost two decades, it seemed their swan song (there is a literal swan on the cover). Unlike *She Hangs Brightly*, the songs are entirely Sandoval and Roback's. Unlike *So Tonight That I Might See*, there are almost no moments when the darkness cracks, when the light seeps into the seams and dispels the notions of moodiness. The album is permeated with death and defeat. It opens with the electric somber "Disappear," which tracks a speaker's inability to vanish and their inability to perform to others' wants. Other standouts "Cry Cry" and "I've Been Let Down" denote efforts to carry on in life after undergoing disappointment. Finally, the album ends on a forlorn beat. In "Look On Down From The Bridge," the singer questions how to say goodbye as she wonders if an unspecified person will come to notice her at the edge of a bridge. It's a far cry from *So Tonight That I Might See*'s urgent call to notice the sunlight piercing through the rain.

Over the years, Sandoval and Roback were adamant their brief success on the charts and public attention did not change their songwriting approach.[26] But no one can deny the money did not disrupt their process. The duo drifted apart, if not by friendship, then by proximity. Sandoval, to work with Roback, rented a home in Berkeley—Roback's favorite city to retreat from the chaos of his career and hometown. Her relationship with William Reid, though, caused her to fall for London. The English capital, cold and rainy, suited her temperament.[27] As "Fade into You" was creating new fans in 1994 and 1995, she insisted on staying in London, requesting to record in the city, and enjoying the separation from the fame-obsessive culture of LA. Roback also enjoyed the gray city and was happy to meet with old touring and recording friends from their Rough Trade days. But whereas Sandoval made London her home, Roback grew restless. He became increasingly nomadic, traveling back to sunny California, stopping somewhere new, and meeting with Sandoval in short bursts to work on new material before the road called him back.[28]

Listening to *Among My Swan* is to listen to this growing separation. It is telling that so many interviews from these years were conducted separately, whether Sandoval or Roback were continents apart or in the same city.[29] *So Tonight That I Might See* is an album about artists defining their hometown. Los Angeles is glitzy and decadent, communal if alienated, and despondent but hopeful. It is an album of two friends coming together to understand how their perspectives on the city compare. In their third album, they have lost this grounding. They have started to lose each other. While she wrote and recorded with Roback, Sandoval appreciated the physical distance and its effect on her writing. She acknowledged that it became harder to record in front of a band, and she enjoyed recording in private and on her own.[30] And so, the album cannot help but replicate their growing isolation.

One of the most intriguing artifacts from this period is the music video for their one single "Flowers in December." Director Kevin Kerslake, who returned after directing "Halah" and the official video for "Fade into You," leads a video that is noticeably higher-budgeted and story-oriented in comparison to their previous releases. In the video, Sandoval wanders through two distinct paths. In one scenario fit for a Tim Burton dreamscape, she holds onto a black Victorian cape as she navigates a foggy landscape intruded upon by desolate, skeletal trees. Shadows of other figures pop in and out. A horse-drawn carriage arrives to transport her. It pulls her along at a frightening speed. Roback appears on a bench before he's gone. Wherever she attempts to go, she arrives at the same spot, stuck behind a tall, locked gate. In the other video's segment, she navigates red hallways in a gorgeous black velvet dress. Eventually, she comes across a door which leads out into the cold, gray landscape. In every scenario, she appears uncomfortably out of place, miserably forced to perform. The song, which may not be the finest of the album, plays on, describing the anger, remorse, and brutal pleasure of letting someone who loves you down.

If I am describing the video in excruciating detail, it is because the video is so rarely seen, even by the Mazzy Star faithful. It is also because it is one of the few moments in which one wonders if the band relinquished a bit of control. After all, Capitol Records relented on typical promotion for *Among My Swan*. They accepted Roback and Sandoval's request for limited press, and they did not force a big-time producer as they wanted. One can almost hear teeth grinding when Clark Staub, then the senior director of marketing at Capitol Records, admitted to *Billboard* that it "is not a trendy album."[31] The video would be the one piece of promotion the marketers had at their disposal. Therefore, a paranoiac might watch the video and check off a list of all the ingredients executives desired from the beginning: lovely portrayals of Sandoval and scenes seemingly fit for Sad Girls to fawn over. About the end of their time with the major label, Sandoval stated Capitol Records "had a formula and suddenly, all these people wanted to . . . make sure we followed that formula."[32]

It's hard to argue that the choice of single wasn't entirely successful. "Flowers in December" charted on the UK singles chart and found minor success on college airwaves. But it also is not hard to understand why the single did not perform better. Interest in Mazzy Star derived from their authenticity to themselves. To force and formulize an aesthetic out of marketing interests or fan desires deprived their music of its dream-inducing enchantment. It robbed listeners of a chance to focus on the set of songs. At the end of the video, Sandoval sings, "And I've been wondering why you let me down / and I've been taking it all for granted."[33] The confession feels directed to two sets of people. For us fans, we should never have expected the band to become something it was not. For Sandoval and Roback, the experience and reward of being able to write their songs and record them to their desires was not an experience they'd ever forget. They would never again give up such control.

Their promotion of *Among My Swan* came to an end in 1997. Fittingly, Mazzy Star played their final shows of the tour in Los Angeles. These were two intimate venues not far from many of the defunct bars and coffeehouses where Roback and Sandoval first started. It was late in March. Spring was coming. The band were not prepared for the season. They were better suited for the winter months, when one does not need an excuse to stay inside and hide from people. They needed to get away and were not ready to step back into the corporate ring of record and tour, and record and tour, with no end in sight. They again approached the executives at Capitol Records. Mazzy Star's reticence at the commercial expectations of the music industry exasperated executives. Sandoval and Roback got what they wanted. They were released from their contract.

Conclusion

For seventeen long and silent years after 1996's *Among My Swan*, it seemed Mazzy Star was over. Hope Sandoval had started a new project entitled Hope Sandoval and the Warm Inventions with My Bloody Valentine's Colm Ó Cíosóig. The duo released albums *Bavarian Fruit Bread* and *Through the Devil Softly* in 2001 and 2009. When not working on her own music, she lent her vocals to disparate genre acts such as the Chemical Brothers, Bert Jansch, and Massive Attack. As ever before, Sandoval remained guarded in interviews. When pushed for more information on the state of Mazzy Star, she avoided discussing the band's future. For that matter, she also avoided the past, refusing to give in to a warm nostalgia. The Warm Inventions was a new project that allowed her to experiment in new directions. It was an opportunity to mellow to a whisper the buzz which followed her in Mazzy Star.[1] Meanwhile, the aughts were a quiet period for Roback. He settled down in London and then in Norway's Oslo. What drew him to the Scandinavian capital is a bit unclear. Scatterings of interviews throughout the years indicate he enjoyed the long winters, an apartment which overlooked a park, and his own recording studio where he stocked Françoise Hardy records he listened to on repeat.[2] An anomaly came in 2004 when Roback provided a cameo as himself for Olivier Assayas's *Clean*, appearing opposite Hong Kong superstar Maggie Cheung whose character sings two original songs of his written specifically for the film. Echoes of Mazzy Star and Opal's dreamscapes can be heard. Otherwise, most of these years were spent creating art in isolation and occasionally giving music away for art installations.

What brought Mazzy Star out of their lengthy hiatus? When asked about it on the onset of their surprising 2013 release *Seasons of Your Day*, the members cloaked the answer with suggestions of indifference about public attention to their art. They asserted repeatedly they were always writing when the rest of the world assumed they were silent. They compared themselves to sculptors and novelists who ignore the public's want for endless content.[3] There is, likely, some truth to each of these responses. At the same time, this is a band who has openly fretted about their tendency to get bored with the recording process. In other words, once a song felt complete, they hurried to finish it in the studio before they lost interest.[4] Stories circulating about the album's creation suggest, however, that Roback and Sandoval were returning to complete unfinished material. While magazines proclaimed it the first original material in almost two decades, several songs on the album were performed or leaked in the early 1990s. Regardless of which tracks were new or simply refined, the overall effect is that of a small miracle. Listen to the album, and Mazzy Star have not missed a beat. Had it been released after *She Hangs Brightly* or after *So Tonight That I Might See*, it would not have appeared unfitting to

CONCLUSION

the thematic concerns which carry from each album. Time was and is irrelevant to Mazzy Star's creations. But time, I wonder, did matter to Roback and Sandoval.

Roback was always the shadow behind Sandoval's uncomfortable push into the spotlight. The tall and skinny man lingered in the dark, illuminated when the light bounced off his guitar, and more often hidden with a beret and sunglasses. As he had done in interviews and to record executives, he seemed ready to support Sandoval should she wilt from attention. There is a sad reversal to this relationship in their 2013 music video "California." Drenched in a heavy black coat and wearing a thick beanie, Roback cannot hide an almost skeletal appearance. Beside Sandoval, he seems to have shrunk to her height. Unlike their other videos, there is no story and no evocation of surrealism. It's all about the two of them, two friends wandering onto and behind a stage. In an interview with *Dazed*, Sandoval describes how "California" was written for her old friend Sylvia Gomez.[5] The song expresses a want to return to the state and a want to reunite with former friends who have faded by distance and time. It's a melancholy piece about bridging these barriers before it is too late. Toward the video's end, Roback and Sandoval are on a rooftop in an undisclosed neighborhood within their home state, watching the sunset as the visuals grow gray. Only Sandoval turns back, and Roback stares on. One wonders if Roback was also on Sandoval's mind when she penned the lyrics?

David Roback died on February 24, 2020. His family reported the cause was metastatic cancer. Friends reported to the *Los Angeles Times* that they had no clue he was sick.

Roback, as he had always done, managed to keep so much of his personal life private. How long he lived with cancer remains unknown except to a select few. Though one wonders if the release of *Seasons of Your Day* let slip that his battle with the illness had already begun? If the video contains the sad and early clues of a struggle? In 2013, while promoting the new album to *Newsweek*, he was asked what he had been up to while Sandoval kept busy with side projects and steady guest vocals. Roback responded, "I did a song for the Norwegian Cancer Society that was quite satisfying."[6] He did not clarify the thought.

In the years and days leading up to his death, Roback alluded to the posthumous releases and remasters of recordings from his long career. Susanna Hoffs described a text from him about their reissuing the out-of-print *Rainy Day*, their cover album featuring Paisley Underground all-stars. To his old friend and Opal bandmate, Kendra Smith, he discussed with her manager and producer Pat Thomas the process of reissuing Opal's albums. Smith and Thomas exchanged emails with Roback agreeing to do so, and lamented Roback's slow and meticulous responses, which delayed the affair. Upon hearing the news, Thomas wondered if Roback had purposely slowed the process, controlling the production to his satisfaction but not wanting to live to see their rerelease. Then there is a question about Mazzy Star. Over the years, Sandoval and Roback hinted that a trove of unreleased music was hidden away, collecting dust. Five years before his death, the pair hinted that they already possessed a plan to leave this archive to their families, who would let the world hear it all only when the two were long

CONCLUSION

dead.[7] Of course, it would not be Mazzy Star if they did not offer some constraint. When asked if this would happen, Sandoval uttered the dreaded word: "probably."[8]

But until that day comes—if it ever comes—we live in a present in which Sandoval has continued to create music. Since *Seasons of Your Day*, she has released a new album with the Warm Inventions. New collaborations with Massive Attack emerged, along with the Psychic Ills and Dirt Blue Gene. Seeing Mazzy Star's influence reach a younger generation, she invited Kurt Vile to feature on the Warm Inventions' single "Let Me Get There." In 2022, Warren Ellis, an Australian composer who is best known for his collaborations with Nick Cave and the Bad Seeds, tweeted that he visited Sandoval in the studio to work on new tracks.[9] So far, nothing has emerged. Perhaps the most interesting update came in the spring of 2024 when *Glen Campbell Duets: Ghost on the Canvas Sessions* appeared. On an album which reimagines the late country act's farewell songs by pairing him with singers across generations, Sandoval's name quietly emerged on the despondent "The Long Walk Home." In the press release, Campbell's producer and songwriting partner Julian Raymond described the late country star's awe for Sandoval's voice after listening to "Mary of Silence."[10] Sandoval, who long sought to provide a feminine edge to the county acts of her childhood, sings perfectly with a ghost. Harmony between the living and a phantom recalls Mark Fisher's claim that certain music consumed by haunting—by the hauntological—evokes "what once was, what could have been, and . . . what could still happen."[11] Her hypnotic singing style is without specific definition, haunting the deepest recesses of our minds, and it suggest certain songs and certain singers can call upon the best of our dead. In the end, we are left wondering where Sandoval's musical journey will lead us next. Toward new interpretations of the past? Toward sonic sounds unimaginable except to those blessed to hear them in the future?

As for Mazzy Star without Roback? It doesn't seem right to hear the band name again if Roback is not there to play guitar. Roback and Sandoval are Mazzy Star. Without one, the heart which sustains the band ceases to beat. A week after Roback's death, Hope Sandoval posted an official message on the group's Facebook page. She included a farewell poem to her friend and described that somehow, without him, the world is "filled with the comforting sadness that holds us together."[12] It's a lovely goodbye and a testament to the band's ability to understand that people can possess contradictory emotions. That sadness is calming. It is the emotion which brings one closer to what one had and what one lost. Sadness is, in short, an excuse to dream again.

If you will allow me a literary reference, Roback and Sandoval are the Don Quixote and Sancho Panza of music. Just as these immortal characters do, they understand the necessity of dreaming to make it through the mundanity of reality. Together, they live in their personal world, building fantasies through song and giving us in their releases a glimpse of their reveries. However dark these worlds are; however bright they appear; and however difficult it is to maintain the stillness required to fade into their creations, for the brief moments we do, it's a beautiful feeling. For me, *So Tonight That I Might See* is the perfect album of theirs

CONCLUSION

which evokes "comforting sadness."[13] It is an excuse to become reacquainted with the melancholia strand of living when I might see what sad news goes on across my city or the globe and not mind drifting off toward *The Twilight Zone*. I hope such an album exists for you. If not, Mazzy Star's music awaits whenever a fantasy is needed, pulling us into a dreamy realm and giving us the space to access the power of the surreal and strange.

References

? (Question Mark) and the Mysterians. "Billboard Hot 100." *Billboard*. www.billboard.com/artist/question-mark-the-mysterians/.

? (Question Mark) interviewed by Mark Wedel. "'Mysterians' Frontman Faces Some Questions from His Past." *Michigan Live*, May 3, 2007. https://www.mlive.com/kalamazoo_gazette_extra/2007/05/mysterians_frontman_faces_some.html.

Alternative Press. "Tangled Up in Blue." *Alternative Press,* Issue #99, November 1996.

Anderson, Susan M. "Valley of Gold: Susan M. Anderson on Southern California and the Phantasmagoric." *Kasmingallery Review*, August 30, 2023. https://review.kasmingallery.com/weekend-long-reads/valley-of-gold-susan-m-anderson-on-southern-california-and-the-phantasmagoric/.

Appleford, Steve. "She's Returning, but Not to the Spotlight." *Los Angeles Times*, October 18, 2009. https://www.latimes.com/archives/la-xpm-2009-oct-18-ca-hope-sandoval18-story.html.

The Bangles. *Different Light*. Columbia Records. 1986.

Billboard. "Billboard Hot 100." *Billboard*. https://www.billboard.com/artist/mazzy-star/.

Blackwell, Mark. "Mild at Heart, Mazzy Star Shines Softly." *Huh*, Issue #4, December 1994.

REFERENCES

Bonner, Michael. "A Mazzy Star Interview: 'There's Happiness, but There's Also Torture...'—Uncut." *Uncut*, February 26, 2020. https://www.uncut.co.uk/features/a-mazzy-star-interview-theres-happiness-but-theres-also-torture-67963/.

Breihan, Tom. "Glen Campbell & Hope Sandoval—'The Long Walk Home.'" *Stereogum,* March 15, 2024. https://www.stereogum.com/2255807/glen-campbell-hope-sandoval-the-long-walk-home/music/.

Breton, André. *Manifestoes of Surrealism*. Translated by Richard Seaver and Helen R. Lane. Ann Arbor: University of Michigan Press, 2010.

Broome, Eric. "Star Light, Star Bright: Eric Broome Sees What Makes Mazzy Star Shine." *Strobe Magazine*, January 1997.

Butler Will. "Hope Sandoval's Influences." *Dazed,* September 23, 2013. https://www.dazeddigital.com/music/article/17233/1/hope-sandovals-influences.

Cartwright, Garth. "Love Guitarist Johnny Echols: 'Arthur Lee Was Warm, Giving—and Obnoxious.'" *Guardian*, July 4, 2022. https://www.theguardian.com/music/2022/jul/04/love-guitarist-johnny-echols-arthur-lee-was-warm-giving-and-obnoxious.

Caulfield, Keith. "Madonna's 40 Biggest Billboard Hits." *Billboard,* August 16, 2024. https://www.billboard.com/lists/madonnas-40-biggest-billboard-hits/.

Chakraborty, Ranjani, and Melissa Hirsch. "Dodger Stadium's Violent Origin Story." *Vox,* May 17, 2021. https://www.vox.com/videos/2021/5/17/22439387/dodger-stadium-chavez-ravine-history.

Chandler, Jenna. "LA 'Sterilized' its Streets for the '84 Olympics—How Will It Treat the Homeless in 2028?" *Curbed*, July 12, 2018. https://la.curbed.com/2018/7/12/17454676/los-angeles-olympics-homeless-police-militarization-security.

REFERENCES

Chonin, Neva. "A New Hope Rises: Mazzy Star's Sandoval Makes a Solo Statement." *San Francisco Chronicle,* October 28, 2001. https://www.hopesandoval.com/press/BFB-sfchronicle.shtml.

Christenson, Camille. "The 1968 East LA Walkouts and the Sorry State of US Education." *Interzine,* August 11, 2021. https://interzineorg.wordpress.com/2021/08/11/the-1968-east-la-walkouts-and-the-sorry-state-of-us-education/.

Cobain, Kurt. *Journals*. New York: Riverhead Books, 2003.

Cohen, Alina. "How Surrealism Changed Los Angeles Forever." *Artsy,* April 17, 2020. https://www.artsy.net/article/artsy-editorial-surrealism-changed-los-angeles-forever.

Cost, Jud. "Mazzy Star: At the Dentist." *The Bob Mag,* Issue #47, Winter 1994.

Dalí, Salvador, quoted in Monica Fernandez. "Mexico: A Surrealist Country." *Fusion Magazine,* October 27, 2015. https://www.fusionmagazine.org/mexico-a-surrealist-country/.

Davis, Erik. "Lysergic Garage Party." *Spin,* March 1989, 16.

Deer, Patrick. "'The Cassette Played Poptones': Punk's Pop Embrace of the City in Ruins." *Social Text* 31, no. 3 (September 1, 2013): 147–58. https://doi.org/10.1215/01642472-2152891.

The Doors. "Break on Through (To the Other Side)." On *The Doors*. Elektra Records, 1967.

Drechsler, Clara. "Opal." *Spex,* no. 6 (June 1988): 21.

duBrowa, Corey. "One Nation Underground: The Story of the Paisley Underground." *Magnet Magazine,* May 18, 2001. https://magnetmagazine.com/2001/05/18/one-nation-underground-the-story-of-the-paisley-underground/.

Duersten, Matthew. "Halfway Between Watts and Charles Manson: Local Idol Arthur Lee." *Los Angeles Magazine,* January 25, 2023. https://lamag.com/news/halfway-between-watts-and-charles-manson-local-idol-arthur-lee.

REFERENCES

Editor, Undisclosed. "Interview with William Reid." *Rockin' On Japan*, August 1995.

Editors. "Interview with Hope Sandoval, Mazzy Star." *POP*, Issue #21, December 1996.

Ellis, Bret Easton. "Beautiful Noise with Susanna Hoffs." *The Bret Easton Ellis Podcast*, season 8, episode 23, June 24, 2024. Audio: 4:30.

Employment Development Department California. "Labor Market Info: 1976-2024." State of California. https://labormarketinfo.edd.ca.gov.

Fisher, Mark. "London After the Rave: Burial." In *Ghosts of My Life: Writings on Depression, Hauntology and Lost Futures*. 98, Winchester, United Kingdom: Zero Books, 2013.

Foege, Alec. "Incense and Insolence Mazzy Star Carry the Torch for '60s Psychedelia and the Importance of Being Difficult." *Rolling Stone,* October 20, 1994.

Frost, Danny. "Constellation Prize." *NME*, October 9, 1993.

Garcia-Furtdao, Laia. "The Joy of Sad Girl Music." *Harper's Bazaar,* February 9, 2022. https://www.harpersbazaar.com/culture/features/a38647867/the-joy-of-sad-girl-music-february-2022/.

Gavan, David. "The Mother of Warm Invention: A Hope Sandoval Interview." *The Quietus*, December 29, 2009. https://thequietus.com/interviews/the-mother-of-warm-invention-a-hope-sandoval-interview/.

Gopalan, Nisha. "Mazzy Star Reunites After 17 Years With New Album, 'Seasons of Your Day.'" *Newsweek*, September 20, 2013. https://www.newsweek.com/2013/09/20/mazzy-star-reunites-after-17-years-new-album-seasons-of-your-day-237998.html.

Greer, Jim. "Mazzy Star in 'Singer Speaks' Shock." *Ray Gun,* Issue #41, November 1996.

Ham, Robert. "Los Lobos: 'La Bamba' Gave us an Identity Crisis." *Guardian*, August 3, 2021. https://www.theguardian.com/music/2021/aug/03/los-lobos-la-bamba-gave-us-an-identity-crisis.

REFERENCES

Hann, Michael. "The Paisley Underground: Los Angeles's 1980s Psychedelic Explosion." *Guardian*, May 16, 2013. https://www.theguardian.com/music/2013/may/16/paisley-underground-history-80s-los-angeles-psychedelia.

Hilburn, Robert. "Mazzy Star: Shining 'Brightly': The Personal Visions of David Roback and Hope Sandoval have Fueled a Fast-moving Album on the Alternative-Rock Charts." *The Los Angeles Times,* July 22, 1990.

Howe, Zoë. *The Jesus and Mary Chain: Barbed Wire Kisses*, 190. New York: St. Martin's Press, 2014.

Hultkrans, Andrew. *Forever Changes*. New York: Bloomsbury Academic, 2013.

Koskoff, Ellen. *Music Cultures in the United States: An Introduction*, 359. New York: Routledge, 2005.

The Jesus and Mary Chain. *Psychocandy*. Blanco y Negro, 1985.

Lee Arthur, quoted in David Stubbs. "Arthur Lee: March 7, 1945—August 3, 2006—Uncut." *Uncut*, November 19, 2019. https://www.uncut.co.uk/features/arthur-lee-march-7-1945-august-3-2006-43374/.

Leng, Karen. "Double J Radio." Australian Broadcasting Corporation, June 12, 2018. Audio 09:18.

Los Angeles County. "Los Angeles County Sheriff's Department—Department Crime Statistics 1960–2012." Los Angeles County Sheriff's Department News Advisory. https://file.lacounty.gov/SDSInter/lasd/189076_LASD-Stats1960-2012.pdf.

Love. "Andmoreagain." On *Forever Changes*. Elektra Records, 1967.

Love. "The Red Telephone." On *Forever Changes*. Elektra Records, 1967.

Lynskey, Dorian. "Mazzy Star: We Weren't Really in the Mood to Release Music.'" *Guardian,* September 19, 2013. https://www.theguardian.com/music/2013/sep/19/mazzy-star-seasons-of-your-day-interview.

REFERENCES

Machado, Yolanda. "La Bamba: American Dreaming, Chicano Style." The Criterion Collection, September 26, 2023. https://www.criterion.com/current/posts/8267-la-bamba-american-dreaming-chicano-style.

Mazzy Star. "Blue Flower." On *She Hangs Brightly*. Rough Trade Records, 1990.

Mazzy Star. "Blue Light." On *So Tonight That I Might See*. Capitol Records, 1993.

Mazzy Star. "Bells Ring." On *So Tonight That I Might See*. Capitol Records, 1993.

Mazzy Star. "Fade Into You." On *So Tonight That I Might See*. Capitol Records, 1993.

Mazzt Star. "Flowers in December." On *Among My Swan*. Capitol Records, 1996.

Mazzy Star. "Ghost on the Highway." On *She Hangs Brightly*. Rough Trade Records, 1990.

Mazzy Star. "She's My Baby." On *So Tonight That I Might See*. Capitol Records, 1993.

Mazzy Star. "So Tonight That I Might See." On *So Tonight That I Might See*. Capitol Records, 1993.

Mazzy Star. "Unreflected." On *So Tonight That I Might See*. Capitol Records, 1993.

Mejia, Paula. "Mazy Star, Out of the Fjord." *Interview*, September 23, 2013. https://www.interviewmagazine.com/music/mazzy-star-seasons-of-your-day.

Mendheim, Beverly. *Ritchie Valens: The First Latino Rocker*. Tempe, Arizona: Bilingual Press/Editorial Bilingüe, 1987.

Mirkin, Steve. "Mazzy Star Shines on Third Album Long-Term Development Key for Capitol Act." *Billboard*, September 21, 1996, 12.

Mize, Ronald, and Alicia Swords. "Operation Wetback, 1954." In *Consuming Mexican Labor: From the Bracero Program to NAFTA*. Ontario, Canada: University of Toronto Press, 2011.

REFERENCES

Moreland, Quinn. "Mazzy Star: *So Tonight That I Might See* Review." *Pitchfork*, November 16, 2018. https://pitchfork.com/reviews/albums/mazzy-star-so-tonight-that-i-might-see/.

Myers, Caren. "Lucky Star." *Details*, December, 1994.

Myers, Paul. "Susanna Hoffs, Down in the Valley, Music Millenium." *The Record Store Day Podcast with Paul Myers*, April 7, 2020. Audio: 35:40. https://myerspodcasting.libsyn.com/susanna-hoffs-down-in-the-valley-music-millenium.

Nash, Ed. "Nine Songs Susanna Hoffs." *The Line of Best Fit*, June 23, 2023, 13:00, https://www.thelineofbestfit.com/features/interviews/nine-songs-susanna-hoffs.

The O.C. "The Escape." Fox, September 16, 2003.

Opal. *Happy Nightmare Baby*. SST. 1987.

Parnell, Annie. "Meditations on Mazzy Star: Growing Up with *So Tonight That I Might See*." *Paste*, October 5, 2023, 10:00AM. https://www.pastemagazine.com/music/mazzy-star/mazzy-star-so-tonight-that-i-might-see-30th-anniversary-essay.

Pons, Joan. "Mazzy Star." *Rock de Lux*, no. 137 (January 1997): 11.

Rain Parade. "What's She Done to Your Mind." On *Emergency Third Rail Power Trip*. Enigma, 1983.

Rajotte, Claude. *Musique Plus*. Montreal, Canada, October 28, 1994.

Rayner, Alex. "Man Ray in L.A.: What Happened When the Pioneering Artist Hit Hollywood." *Guardian*, January 16, 2018. https://www.theguardian.com/artanddesign/2018/jan/16/man-ray-in-la-what-happened-when-the-pioneering-artist-hit-hollywood.

Reisman, Abraham Josephine. "Is Mazzy Star's 'Fade Into You' the Most Overused Song in Film and TV?" *Vulture*, October 1, 2013. https://www.vulture.com/2013/09/overused-song-mazzy-star-fade-into-you.html.

Ricketts, Paul. "A Sense of Detachment." *Unhinged*, Issue #7, November 1990.

REFERENCES

Roberts, Michael. "The Quiet Man." *Westword,* March 30, 1994. https://www.westword.com/music/the-quiet-man-5053835.

Roberts, Randall. "Mazzy Star's David Roback Remembered by Susanna Hoffs and Friends—Los Angeles Times." *Los Angeles Times*, March 9, 2020. https://www.latimes.com/entertainment-arts/music/story/2020-03-06/david-roback-mazzy-star-susanna-hoffs-opal-cancer.

The Rolling Stones. "Goin' Home." On *Aftermath*. ABKO Music and Records, 1966.

Ruiz, Matthew Ismael. "Revisiting La Bamba, the Ritchie Valens Biopic That Underscores the Myth of the American Dream." *Pitchfork,* August 27, 2020. https://pitchfork.com/thepitch/revisiting-la-bamba-the-ritchie-valens-biopic-that-underscores-the-myth-of-the-american-dream/.

Salik, Yasi, and Meaghan Garvey. "Mazzy Star with Meaghan Garvey." *Bandsplain*, The Ringer, November 2, 2023. Audio 30:52. https://www.theringer.com/podcasts/bandsplain/2023/11/02/mazzy-star-with-meaghan-garvey.

Sandoval, Hope. "It's been a Few Days since I Lost My Dear Friend…" *Facebook*, March 1, 2020. https://www.facebook.com/photo.php?fbid=2793746304045083&id=480887555330981&set=a.487710271315376.

Shea, Erik. "Magick Power: Introducing Hope Sandoval and the Warm Inventions." *East Bay Express,* November 7, 2001. https://eastbayexpress.com/magick-power-1/.

Soffer, Jonathan. "Introduction." In *Ed Koch and the Rebuilding of New York City*, 1–11. Columbia University Press, 2010. http://www.jstor.org/stable/10.7312/soff15032.4.

Sonic Youth. *Goo.* DGC Records. 1990.

Sonic Youth. *Dirty*. DGC Records. 1992.

Soutar, Elise. "Warren Ellis Teases New Collaboration with Hope Sandoval." *Paste*, January 24, 2022. https://www.pastemagazine

REFERENCES

.com/music/warren-ellis/warren-ellis-teases-hope-sandoval-collaboration.

True, Everett. "Give 'Em Enough Hope Mazzy Star.'" *Melody Maker*, January 5, 1991.

True, Everett. "Mazzy Star: Ghost Riders in the Sky." *Melody Maker,* June 9, 1990.

Tures, Daniel. "Remembering David Roback and L.A.'s Paisley Underground Scene." *Los Angeles Public Library Blog*, March 9, 2020. https://www.lapl.org/collections-resources/blogs/lapl/remembering-david-roback-and-la-paisley-underground-scene.

Warren, Bruce. "Mazzy Star." *Option*, January 1991.

Waxman, Olivia B. "30 Years After the Rodney King Verdict, Why Advocates Believe 'Reforms Didn't Go Far Enough.'" *Time*, April 29, 2022. https://time.com/6169564/rodney-king-riots-beating-anniversary/.

Weir, James. "Story behind Mazzy Star's Sleepy '90s Hit Fade Into You." *Nationwide News Australia*, June 12, 2018. https://www.news.com.au/entertainment/music/tours/story-behind-mazzy-stars-sleepy-90s-hit-fade-into-you/news-story/b688af65c0399cd5030e5d4956b75227.

Wild, David. "L.A. Confidential." *Rolling Stone,* no. 664, Setember 1993.

Wolf, Erika. "Mazzy Star's 'So Tonight That I Might See' Turns 30." *Albumism*, October 1, 2023. https://albumism.com/features/mazzy-star-so-tonight-that-i-might-see-album-anniversary.

Wolf, Jessica. "East L.A. Chicano Student Walkouts: 50 Years Later." UCLA, March 9, 2018. https://newsroom.ucla.edu/stories/east-l-a-chicano-student-walkouts:-50-years-later.

Wolkoff, Joanie. "Fragility and Strength: Cracking Hope Sandoval and the Warm Inventions." *Vice*, November 8, 2016. https://www.vice.com/en/article/fragility-and-strength-cracking-hope-sandoval-and-the-warm-inventions/.

REFERENCES

Woods, Karen. "Mazzy Star." *Ray Gun,* Issue #12, December/January 1993.

Zimmerman, Lee. "If She Knew What She Wants: Susanna Hoffs at 65, Celebrating the Brilliance of a Power Pop Icon." *Rock and Roll Globe*, January 17, 2024. https://rockandrollglobe.com/power-pop/if-she-knew-what-she-wants-susanna-hoffs-at-65/.

Notes

Introduction

1 Hope Sandoval, quoted in D. Wild, "L.A. Confidential," *Rolling Stone*, no. 664 (September 1993): 28.

2 Alternative Press, "Tangled Up in Blue," *Alternative Press*, Issue #99, November 1996.

Chapter 1

1 André Breton, *Manifestoes of Surrealism* (Ann Arbor: University of Michigan Press, 2010), 26.

2 Salvador Dalí, quoted in Monica Fernandez, "Mexico: A Surrealist Country," *Fusion Magazine*, October 27, 2015. https://www.fusionmagazine.org/mexico-a-surrealist-country/.

3 David Roback and Hope Sandoval, Mazzy Star, "Fade into You," on *So Tonight That I Might See*, Capitol Records, 1993.

4 Roback and Sandoval, Mazzy Star, "Fade into You."

5 Eric Broome, "Star Light, Star Bright: Eric Broome Sees What Makes Mazzy Star Shine," *Strobe Magazine*, January 1997.

NOTES

6   Quinn Moreland, "Mazzy Star: *So Tonight That I Might See* Review," *Pitchfork*, November 16, 2018. https://pitchfork.com/reviews/albums/mazzy-star-so-tonight-that-i-might-see/.

7   David Roback, interviewed by J. Weir, "Story behind Mazzy Star's Sleepy '90s Hit Fade into You," *Nationwide News Australia*, June 12, 2018. https://www.news.com.au/entertainment/music/tours/story-behind-mazzy-stars-sleepy-90s-hit-fade-into-you/news-story/b688af65c0399cd5030e5d4956b75227.

8   Abraham Josephine Reisman, "Is Mazzy Star's 'Fade into You' the Most Overused Song in Film and TV?" *Vulture*, October 1, 2013. https://www.vulture.com/2013/09/overused-song-mazzy-star-fade-into-you.html.

9   Roback and Sandoval, Mazzy Star, "Fade into You."

10 David Roback, interviewed by E. True, "Mazzy Star: Ghost Riders in the Sky," *Melody Maker,* June 9, 1990.

11 Susan M. Anderson, "Valley of Gold: Susan M. Anderson on Southern California and the Phantasmagoric," *Kasmingallery Review*, August 30, 2023. https://review.kasmingallery.com/weekend-long-reads/valley-of-gold-susan-m-anderson-on-southern-california-and-the-phantasmagoric/.

12 Man Ray, quoted in Alex Rayner, "Man Ray in L.A.: What Happened When the Pioneering Artist Hit Hollywood," *Guardian*, January 16, 2018. https://www.theguardian.com/artanddesign/2018/jan/16/man-ray-in-la-what-happened-when-the-pioneering-artist-hit-hollywood.

13 Roback and Sandoval, Mazzy Star, "Fade into You."

14 The Doors, "Break on Through (To the Other Side)," on *The Doors*, Elektra Records, 1967.

NOTES

15 David Roback, Mazzy Star, "Ghost on the Highway," on *She Hangs Brightly,* Rough Trade Records, 1990.

16 David Roback and Hope Sandoval, Mazzy Star, "So Tonight That I Might See," on *So Tonight That I Might See*, Capitol Records, 1993.

17 David Roback, quoted in E. True, "Give 'Em Enough Hope Mazzy Star," *Melody Maker*, January 5, 1991, 33.

18 David Roback, quoted in M. Bonner, "A Mazzy Star Interview," *Uncut*, April 24, 2015. https://www.uncut.co.uk/features/a-mazzy-star-interview-theres-happiness-but-theres-also-torture-67963/.

19 Susanna Hoffs, quoted in R. Roberts, "Susanna Hoffs and Friends Remember David Roback, Who Stayed Creative, and Enigmatic to the End," *Los Angeles Times,* March 6, 2020. https://www.latimes.com/entertainment-arts/music/story/2020-03-06/david-roback-mazzy-star-susanna-hoffs-opal-cancer.

20 David Roback, quoted in J. Cost, "Mazzy Star: At the Dentist," *The Bob Mag*, Issue #47, Winter 1994.

21 Arthur Lee, quoted in D. Stubbs, "Arthur Lee: March 7, 1945—August 3, 2006," *Uncut*, August 4, 2006. https://www.uncut.co.uk/features/arthur-lee-march-7-1945-august-3-2006-43374/.

22 Johnny Echols, quoted in G. Cartwright, "Love guitarist Johnny Echols: 'Arthur Lee was Warm, Giving—and Obnoxious,'" *Guardian*, July 4, 2022. https://www.theguardian.com/music/2022/jul/04/love-guitarist-johnny-echols-arthur-lee-was-warm-giving-and-obnoxious.

23 Andrew Hultkrans, *Forever Changes* (New York: Bloomsbury Academic, 2013), 4.

NOTES

24 Johnny Echols, *Guardian*.

25 Arthur Lee, Love, "The Red Telephone," on *Forever Changes*, Elektra Records, 1967.

26 Arthur Lee, Love, "Andmoreagain," on *Forever Changes*, Elektra Records, 1967.

27 Arthur Lee, Love, "Andmoreagain."

28 Roback, David, quoted in True, "Mazzy Star: Ghost Riders in the Sky."

29 Roback and Sandoval, Mazzy Star, "Fade into You."

Chapter 2

1 Beverly Mendheim, *Ritchie Valens: The First Latino Rocker* (Bilingual Press/Editorial Bilingüe, 1987), 19.

2 Yolanda Machado, "*La Bamba*: American Dreaming, Chicano Style," *Criterion Collection*, September 26, 2023. https://www.criterion.com/current/posts/8267-la-bamba-american-dreaming-chicano-style.

3 Machado, "*La Bamba*: American Dreaming, Chicano Style."

4 Mendheim, *Ritchie Valens: The First Latino Rocker* (Bilingual Press/Editorial Bilingüe, 1987), 22.

5 Alicia Swords and Ronald Mize, "Operation Wetback," in *Consuming Mexican Labor: From the Bracero Program to NAFTA* (Ontario, Canada: University of Toronto Press, 2011), 25.

6 Swords and Mize, "Operation Wetback."

7 Ranjani Chakraborty and Melissa Hirsch, "Dodger Stadium's Violent Origin Story," *Vox*, May 17, 2021. https://www.vox.com/videos/2021/5/17/22439387/dodger-stadium-chavez-ravine-history.

NOTES

8 Question Mark, interviewed by M. Wedel, "Mysterians Frontman Faces Some Questions from His Past," *Michigan Live,* May 3, 2007. https://www.mlive.com/kalamazoo_gazette_extra/2007/05/mysterians_frontman_faces_some.html.

9 Question Mark (?) and the Mysterians, "Billboard Hot 100," *Billboard.* www.billboard.com/artist/question-mark-the-mysterians/.

10 Jessica Wolf, "East L.A. Chicano Student Walkouts: 50 years Later," *UCLA Newsroom*, March 9, 2018. https://newsroom.ucla.edu/stories/east-l-a-chicano-student-walkouts:-50-years-later

11 Camille Christenson, "The 1968 East LA Walkouts and the Sorry State of US Education," *Interzine,* August 11, 2021. https://interzineorg.wordpress.com/2021/08/11/the-1968-east-la-walkouts-and-the-sorry-state-of-us-education/.

12 Christenson, "The 1968 East LA Walkouts and the Sorry State of US Education."

13 Everett True, "Give 'Em Enough Hope, Mazzy Star," *Melody Maker*, January 5, 1991.

14 Hope Sandoval, interviewed by J. Wolkoff, "Fragility and Strength: Cracking Hope Sandoval and the Warm Inventions," *Vice*, November 8, 2016. https://www.vice.com/en/article/fragility-and-strength-cracking-hope-sandoval-and-the-warm-inventions/.

15 Hope Sandoval, interviewed by S. Appleford, "She's Returning, but Not to the Spotlight," *The Los Angeles Times,* October 18, 2009. https://www.latimes.com/archives/la-xpm-2009-oct-18-ca-hope-sandoval18-story.html.

16 Los Angeles County, "Los Angeles County Sheriff's Department—Department Crime Statistics 1960–2012," Los

NOTES

Angeles County Sheriff's Department News Advisory. https://file.lacounty.gov/SDSInter/lasd/189076_LASD-Stats1960-2012.pdf.

17 Employment Development Department California, "Labor Market Info: 1976–2024," State of California. https://labormarketinfo.edd.ca.gov.

18 Hope Sandoval, interviewed by D. Frost, "Constellation Prize." *NME*, October 9, 1993.

19 Sandoval, "Constellation Prize."

20 Hope Sandoval, interviewed by B. Warren, "Mazzy Star," *Option Magazine*, January 1991.

21 Hope Sandoval, interviewed by editors at POP, "Interview with Hope Sandoval, Mazzy Star." *POP*, Issue #21, December 1996.

22 Hope Sandoval, interviewed by P. Ricketts, "Mazzy Star: A Sense of Detachment," *Unhinged Magazine*, Issue #7, November 1990.

23 Sandoval, "Interview with Hope Sandoval, Mazzy Star."

24 Mick Jagger and Keith Richards, The Rolling Stones, "Goin' Home," on *Aftermath*, ABKO Music and Records, 1966.

25 David Roback and Hope Sandoval, Mazzy Star, "She's My Baby," on *So Tonight That I Might See*, Capitol Records, 1993.

26 Keith Caulfield, "Madonna's 40 Biggest Billboard Hits," *Billboard*, August 16, 2024. https://www.billboard.com/lists/madonnas-40-biggest-billboard-hits/.

27 Sandoval, "Mazzy Star: A Sense of Detachment."

28 Hope Sandoval, Interviewed by Karen Woods, "Mazzy Star," *Ray Gun*, Issue # 12, December / January 1993.

NOTES

29 Erika Wolf, "Mazzy Star's 'So Tonight That I Might See' Turns 30," *Albumism*, October 1, 2023. https://albumism.com/features/mazzy-star-so-tonight-that-i-might-see-album-anniversary.

30 Erik Davis, "Lysergic Garage Party," *Spin*, March 1989, 16.

31 Hope Sandoval, interviewed by E. True, "Mazzy Star: Ghost Riders in the Sky," *Melody Maker*, June 9, 1990.

32 David Roback, interviewed by Clara Drechsler, "Opal," *Spex Magazine*, no. 6 (June 1988): 21.

33 David Roback, interviewed by Karen Leng, "Double J Radio," Australian Broadcasting Corporation, June 12, 2018. Audio 09:18.

34 Woods, "Mazzy Star."

35 Hope Sandoval, interviewed by M. Blackwell, "Mild at Heart, Mazzy Star Shines Softly," *Huh Magazine*, Issue #4, December 1994.

36 David Roback and Hope Sandoval, Mazzy Star, "Blue Light," on *So Tonight That I Might See*, Capitol Records, 1993.

37 Roback and Sandoval, Mazzy Star, "Blue Light."

38 Roback and Sandoval, Mazzy Star, "Blue Light."

39 True, "Give 'Em Enough Hope Mazzy Star," 33.

40 Yasi Salek and Meaghan Garvey, "Mazzy Star with Meaghan Garvey," *Bandsplain*, The Ringer, November 2, 2023. Audio 30:52. https://www.theringer.com/podcasts/bandsplain/2023/11/02/mazzy-star-with-meaghan-garvey.

41 Machado, "*La Bamba*: American Dreaming, Chicano Style."

42 Matthew Ismael Ruiz, "Revisiting La Bamba, the Ritchie Valens Biopic That Underscores the Myth of the American Dream," *Pitchfork*, August 27, 2020. https://pitchfork.com/

NOTES

thepitch/revisiting-la-bamba-the-ritchie-valens-biopic-that-underscores-the-myth-of-the-american-dream/.

43 Robert Ham, "Los Lobos: 'La Bamba' Gave us an Identity Crisis," *The Guardian*, August 3, 2021. https://www.theguardian.com/music/2021/aug/03/los-lobos-la-bamba-gave-us-an-identity-crisis.

44 Hope Sandoval, "Interview with Hope Sandoval, Mazzy Star."

45 Hope Sandoval and David Roback, Mazzy Star, "Unreflected," on *So Tonight That I Might See*, Capitol Records, 1993.

46 Sandoval and Roback, Mazzy Star, "Unreflected."

47 Sandoval and Roback, Mazzy Star, "Unreflected."

Chapter 3

1 Robert Hilburn, "Mazzy Star: Shining 'Brightly': The Personal Visions of David Roback and Hope Sandoval have Fueled a Fast-moving Album on the Alternative-Rock Charts," *The Los Angeles Times*, July 22, 1990.

2 Susanna Hoffs, quoted in R. Roberts, "Susanna Hoffs and Friends Remember David Roback, Who Stayed Creative, and Enigmatic to the End," *Los Angeles Times*, March 6, 2020. https://www.latimes.com/entertainment-arts/music/story/2020-03-06/david-roback-mazzy-star-susanna-hoffs-opal-cancer.

3 Matt Piucci, quoted in Roberts, "Susanna Hoffs and Friends Remember David Roback, Who Stayed Creative, and Enigmatic to the End."

4 Jonathan Soffer, "Introduction," in *Ed Koch and the Rebuilding of New York City* (Columbia University Press, 2010), 1–11.

NOTES

5 Patrick Deer, "'The Casette Played Poptones': Punk's Pop Embrace of the City in Ruins," *Social Text* 31, no. 3 (September 1, 2013): 1–11.

6 David Roback, interviewed by Hilburn, "Mazzy Star: Shining 'Brightly.'"

7 Susanna Hoffs, interviewed by B. Easton Ellis, "Beautiful Noise with Susanna Hoffs," *The Bret Easton Ellis Podcast*, season 8, episode 23, June 24, 2024. Audio: 4:30.

8 Susanna Hoffs, quoted in Roberts, "Susanna Hoffs and Friends Remember David Roback, Who Stayed Creative, and Enigmatic to the End."

9 Susanna Hoffs claims to have recordings from this era stashed away in a box. Hoffs, "Susanna Hoffs and Friends Remember David Roback, Who Stayed Creative, and Enigmatic to the End."

10 Susanna Hoffs, interviewed by P. Myers, "Susanna Hoffs, Down in the Valley, Music Millenium," *The Record Store Day Podcast with Paul Myers,* April 7, 2020. Audio: 35:40. https://myerspodcasting.libsyn.com/susanna-hoffs-down-in-the-valley-music-millenium.

11 Lee Zimmerman, "If She Knew What She Wants: Susanna Hoffs at 65, Celebrating the Brilliance of a Power Pop Icon," *Rock and Roll Globe*, January 17, 2024. https://rockandrollglobe.com/power-pop/if-she-knew-what-she-wants-susanna-hoffs-at-65/.

12 Susanna Hoffs, interviewed by E. Nash, "Nine Songs Susanna Hoffs," *The Line of Best Fit*, June 23, 2023, 13:00. https://www.thelineofbestfit.com/features/interviews/nine-songs-susanna-hoffs.

13 Hoffs, "Susanna Hoffs, Down in the Valley, Music Millenium," Audio, 37:35.

NOTES

14 Piucci, "Susanna Hoffs and Friends Remember David Roback, Who Stayed Creative, and Enigmatic to the End."

15 Piucci, "Susanna Hoffs and Friends Remember David Roback, Who Stayed Creative, and Enigmatic to the End."

16 Matt Piucci and David Roback, Rain Parade, "What's She Done to Your Mind," on *Emergency Third Rail Power Trip*, Enigma, 1983.

17 Michael Quercio, interviewed by M. Hann, "The Paisley Underground: Los Angeles's 1980s Psychedelic Explosion," *Guardian*, May 16, 2013. https://www.theguardian.com/music/2013/may/16/paisley-underground-history-80s-los-angeles-psychedelia.

18 Daniel Tures, "Remembering David Roback and L.A.'s Paisley Underground Scene," *Los Angeles Public Library Blog*, March 9, 2020. https://www.lapl.org/collections-resources/blogs/lapl/remembering-david-roback-and-la-paisley-underground-scene.

19 Sid Griffin, interviewed by Hann, "The Paisley Underground: Los Angeles's 1980s Psychedelic Explosion."

20 Michael Quercio, quoted in Corey DuBrowa, "One Nation Underground: The Story of the Paisley Underground," *Magnet Magazine*, May 18, 2001. https://magnetmagazine.com/2001/05/18/one-nation-underground-the-story-of-the-paisley-underground/.

21 Steve Wynn, interviewed by Hann, "The Paisley Underground: Los Angeles's 1980s Psychedelic Explosion."

22 Matt Piucci, interviewed by Hann, "The Paisley Underground: Los Angeles's 1980s Psychedelic Explosion."

23 Steve Wynn, interviewed by Hann, "The Paisley Underground: Los Angeles's 1980s Psychedelic Explosion."

NOTES

24 Vicki Peterson, interviewed by Hann, "The Paisley Underground: Los Angeles's 1980s Psychedelic Explosion."

25 Steve Wynn, interviewed by Hann, "The Paisley Underground: Los Angeles's 1980s Psychedelic Explosion."

26 Matt Piucci, interviewed by Hann, "The Paisley Underground: Los Angeles's 1980s Psychedelic Explosion."

27 Hann, "The Paisley Underground: Los Angeles's 1980s Psychedelic Explosion."

28 Dan Stuart, "The Paisley Underground: Los Angeles's 1980s Psychedelic Explosion."

29 Jenna Chandler, "LA 'Sterilized' its Streets for the '84 Olympics—How Will It Treat the Homeless in 2028?" *Curbed*, July 12, 2018. https://la.curbed.com/2018/7/12/17454676/los-angeles-olympics-homeless-police-militarization-security.

30 Sid Griffin, interviewed by Hann, "The Paisley Underground: Los Angeles's 1980s Psychedelic Explosion."

31 Vicki Peterson, interviewed by Hann, "The Paisley Underground: Los Angeles's 1980s Psychedelic Explosion."

32 Sid Griffin, interviewed by Hann, "The Paisley Underground: Los Angeles's 1980s Psychedelic Explosion."

33 DuBrowa, "One Nation Underground: The Story of the Paisley Underground."

34 Piucci, "Susanna Hoffs and Friends Remember David Roback, Who Stayed Creative, and Enigmatic to the End."

35 Hope Sandoval and Sylvia Gomez recorded at the same studio for Going Home's demo. DuBrowa, "One Nation Underground: The Story of the Paisley Underground."

36 Kendra Smith, interviewed by Hilburn, "Mazzy Star: Shining 'Brightly.'"

NOTES

37 Matt Piucci, interviewed by Hann, "The Paisley Underground: Los Angeles's 1980s Psychedelic Explosion."

38 Hope Sandoval, interviewed by P. Ricketts, "Mazzy Star: A Sense of Detachment," *Unhinged Magazine*, Issue #7, November 1990.

39 Peter Blevgard and Anthony Moore, "Blue Flower," performed by Mazzy Star, on *She Hangs Brightly,* Rough Trade Records, 1990.

40 Kurt Cobain, *Journals* (New York, NY: Riverhead Books, 2003).

41 David Roback and Hope Sandoval, interviewed by D. Frost, "Constellation Prize," *NME*, October 9, 1993.

42 Alec Foege, "Incense and Insolence Mazzy Star Carry the Torch for '60s Psychedelia and the Importance of Being Difficult," *Rolling Stone,* October 20, 1994.

43 Foege, "Incense and Insolence Mazzy Star Carry the Torch for '60s Psychedelia and the Importance of Being Difficult."

44 David Roback, interviewed by J. Greer, "Mazzy Star in 'Singer Speaks' Shock," *Ray Gun,* Issue #41, November 1996.

45 Olivia B. Waxman, "30 Years After the Rodney King Verdict, Why Advocates Believe 'Reforms Didn't Go Far Enough,'" *Time*, April 29, 2022. https://time.com/6169564/rodney-king-riots-beating-anniversary/.

46 Hope Sandoval, interviewed by Frost, "Constellation Prize."

47 David Roback, interviewed by Frost, "Constellation Prize."

Chapter 4

1 Hope Sandoval, quoted in S. Appleford, "She's Returning but not to the Spotlight," *Los Angeles Times*, October 18, 2009.

NOTES

    https://www.latimes.com/archives/la-xpm-2009-oct-18-ca-hope-sandoval18-story.html.

2 Quinn Moreland, "Mazzy Star: *So Tonight That I Might See* Review," *Pitchfork*, November 16, 2018. https://pitchfork.com/reviews/albums/mazzy-star-so-tonight-that-i-might-see/.

3 Steve Mirkin, "Mazzy Star Shines on Third Album Long-Term Development Key for Capitol Act," *Billboard*, September 21, 1996, 12.

4 Annie Parnell, "Meditations on Mazzy Star: Growing Up with *So Tonight That I Might See*," Paste, October 5, 2023, 10:00AM. https://www.pastemagazine.com/music/mazzy-star/mazzy-star-so-tonight-that-i-might-see-30th-anniversary-essay.

5 David Roback and Hope Sandoval, Mazzy Star, "Bells Ring," on *So Tonight That I Might See,* Capitol Records, 1993.

6 Roback and Sandoval, Mazzy Star, "Bells Ring."

7 Roback and Sandoval, Mazzy Star, "Bells Ring."

8 Roback and Sandoval, Mazzy Star, "Bells Ring."

9 David Roback and Hope Sandoval, Mazzy Star, "Mary of Silence," on *So Tonight That I Might See*, Capitol Records, 1993.

10 Hope Sandoval, interviewed by Claude Rajotte, *Musique Plus*, Montreal, Canada, October 28, 1994.

11 David Roback, interviewed by Alternative Press, "Tangled Up in Blue," *Alternative Press,* Issue #99, November 1996.

12 Alternative Press, "Tangled Up in Blue."

13 Laia Garcia-Furtado, "The Joy of Sad Girl Music," *Harper's Bazaar,* February 9, 2022. https://www.harpersbazaar.com/culture/features/a38647867/the-joy-of-sad-girl-music-february-2022/.

NOTES

14 *The O.C,* "The Escape," *Fox*, September 16, 2003.

15 Ellen Koskoff, *Music Cultures in the United States: An Introduction* (New York: Routledge, 2005), 359.

16 Hope Sandoval, interviewed by Rajotte, *Musique Plus*.

17 Zoë Howe, *The Jesus and Mary Chain: Barbed Wire Kisses* (New York: St. Martin's Press, 2014), 190.

18 Howe, *The Jesus and Mary Chain: Barbed Wire Kisses,* 241.

19 Mazzy Star, "Billboard Hot 100," *Billboard*. https://www.billboard.com/artist/mazzy-star/.

20 There is some speculation that Hope Sandoval and William Reid were on and off in their relationship until at least 1996. However, in an interview with the Japanese magazine Rockin' On, William Reid says their relationship ended toward the end of 1994.

William Reid, interviewed by Rockin' On, "Interview with William Reid," *Rockin'On Japan*, August 1995. https://aprilskies.amniisia.com/articles/art_copy.php?id=120&sort=interview.

21 Hope Sandoval, interviewed by E. Shea, "Magick Power: Introducing Hope Sandoval and the Warm Inventions," *East Bay Express,* November 7, 2001. https://eastbayexpress.com/magick-power-1/.

22 Sandoval, "Magick Power: Introducing Hope Sandoval and the Warm Inventions."

23 Colm Ó Cíosóig, "Magick Power: Introducing Hope Sandoval and the Warm Inventions."

24 Hope Sandoval, quoted in Appleford, "She's Returning but not to the Spotlight."

25 David Roback, interviewed by M. Roberts, "The Quiet Man," *Westword,* March 30, 1994. https://www.westword.com/music/the-quiet-man-5053835.

NOTES

26 David Roback, interviewed by E. Broome, "Star Light, Star Bright: Eric Broome Sees What Makes Mazzy Star Shine," *Strobe Magazine*, January 1997.

27 Hope Sandoval, interviewed by J. Greer, "Mazzy Star in 'Singer Speaks' Shock," *Ray Gun,* Issue #41, November 1996.

28 Roback, "Star Light, Star Bright: Eric Broome Sees What Makes Mazzy Star Shine."

29 Roback, "Star Light, Star Bright: Eric Broome Sees What Makes Mazzy Star Shine."

30 Hope Sandoval, interviewed by D. Lynskey, "Mazzy Star: We Weren't Really in the Mood to Release Music,'" *Guardian,* September 19, 2013. https://www.theguardian.com/music/2013/sep/19/mazzy-star-seasons-of-your-day-interview.

31 Clark Staub, quoted in Mirkin, "Mazzy Star Shines on Third Album Long-Term Development Key for Capitol Act," 12.

32 Hope Sandoval, interviewed by N. Chonin, "A New Hope Rises: Mazzy Star's Sandoval Makes a Solo Statement," *San Francisco Chronicle,* October 28, 2001. https://www.hopesandoval.com/press/BFB-sfchronicle.shtml.

33 Hope Sandoval and David Roback, Mazzy Star, "Flowers in December," on *Among My Swan*, Capitol Records, 1996.

Conclusion

1 Hope Sandoval, interviewed by E. Shea, "Magick Power: Introducing Hope Sandoval and the Warm Inventions," *East Bay Express,* November 7, 2001. https://eastbayexpress.com/magick-power-1/.

NOTES

2   David Roback, interviewed by P. Mejia, "Mazy Star, Out of the Fjord," *Interview*, September 23, 2013. https://www.interviewmagazine.com/music/mazzy-star-seasons-of-your-day.

3   David Roback, interviewed by D. Lynskey, "Mazzy Star: We Weren't Really in the Mood to Release Music,'" *Guardian*, September 19, 2013. https://www.theguardian.com/music/2013/sep/19/mazzy-star-seasons-of-your-day-interview.

4   David Roback, interviewed by J. Pons, "Mazzy Star," *Rock de Lux*, no. 137 (January 1997): 11.

5   Hope Sandoval, quoted by Will Butler, "Hope Sandoval's Influences," *Dazed*, September 23, 2013. https://www.dazeddigital.com/music/article/17233/1/hope-sandovals-influences.

6   David Roback, quoted in N. Gopalan, "Mazzy Star Reunites After 17 Years With New Album, 'Seasons of Your Day,'" *Newsweek*, September 20, 2013. https://www.newsweek.com/2013/09/20/mazzy-star-reunites-after-17-years-new-album-seasons-your-day-237998.html.

7   Hope Sandoval, interviewed by M. Bonner, "A Mazzy Star Interview," *Uncut*, April 24, 2015. https://www.uncut.co.uk/features/a-mazzy-star-interview-theres-happiness-but-theres-also-torture-67963/.

8   Hope Sandoval, interviewed by Bonner, "A Mazzy Star Interview."

9   Warren Ellis, quoted in E. Soutar, "Warren Ellis Teases New Collaboration with Hope Sandoval," *Paste*, January 24, 2022. https://www.pastemagazine.com/music/warren-ellis/warren-ellis-teases-hope-sandoval-collaboration.

NOTES

10 Julian Raymond, quoted in T. Breihan, "Glen Campbell & Hope Sandoval—'The Long Walk Home,'" *Stereogum,* March 15, 2024. https://www.stereogum.com/2255807/glen-campbell-hope-sandoval-the-long-walk-home/music/.

11 Mark Fisher, "London After the Rave: Burial," in *Ghosts of My Life: Writings on Depression, Hauntology and Lost Futures* (Winchester, United Kingdom: Zero Books, 2013), 98.

12 Hope Sandoval, "It's been a Few Days Since I Lost My Dear Friend . . . " *Facebook*, March 1, 2020. https://www.facebook.com/photo.php?fbid=2793746304045083&id=480887555330981&set=a.487710271315376.

13 Sandoval, "It's been a Few Days Since I Lost My Dear Friend . . . " *Facebook*.